Critical Guides to Spanish Texts

Critical Guides to Spanish Texts

EDITED BY J.E. VAREY AND A.D. DEYERMOND

PÉREZ DE AYALA

Tigre Juan and
El curandero de su honra

J. J. Macklin

Lecturer in Hispanic Studies
University of Hull

Grant & Cutler Ltd *in association with*
Tamesis Books Ltd 1980

Ⓒ Grant & Cutler Ltd
   1980
ISBN 0 7293 0100-1

I.S.B.N. 84-499-4672-7

DEPÓSITO LEGAL : V. 1.287 - 1981

Printed in Spain by
Artes Gráficas Soler, S.A., Valencia
for
GRANT & CUTLER LTD
11 BUCKINGHAM STREET, LONDON, W.C.2.

Contents

For Helen and Jonathan

References

Except where otherwise indicated, all references to Pérez de Ayala's writings are to the four-volume Aguilar edition of the *Obras completas* and take the form of volume followed by page number. The italic figures in parenthesis refer to numbered items in the Bibliographical Note; the italic figure is followed by a page reference.

I Art and Life

Tigre Juan and *El curandero de su honra*, which is dated 'Riaza (Segovia), septiembre 1925', was first published in two parts in 1926. It is Pérez de Ayala's last full-length novel and earned him the Premio Nacional de Literatura in 1928. Although these works first appeared in separate volumes and with separate titles, neither is complete in itself and in this study they will be treated as a single novel. Most critics, emphasising what Mariano Baquero Goyanes refers to as 'la deformada resonancia tenoriesca en *Tigre Juan*, el trasfondo de parodia calderoniana en *El curandero de su honra*' (*3*, 172), find the novel interesting primarily as an original interpretation of the character of Don Juan and a comic deflation of the Spanish code of honour. Ayala, according to Andrés Amorós, explores 'la vivencia social, española, del amor' (*2*, 359). Naturally one should not underestimate the social relevance of Ayala's ideas on relations between the sexes in the Spain of the 1920s, but that he should have chosen as the subject-matter for his last novel well-known literary themes and interpreted them from a completely new point of view suggests that his aims were at least as much artistic as social. Implicit in Ayala's choice and handling of his material is a probing into the relationship between life and literature, an exploration of the importance of fictions in men's lives and of the value of art in coming to terms with reality. These are characteristically twentieth-century concerns which identify Ayala unmistakably with those contemporary Spanish and European writers who sought to free the novel from the limitations of nineteenth-century Realism.

It is a commonplace of literary history that a significant change took place, in Spain as in other Western countries, in the novel during the early part of this century. The nineteenth-century novel had been dominated by Realism, which can be defined in broad terms as the attempt to reproduce in fiction the conditions, laws and circumstances which are believed to prevail in the real world. There are, of course, many kinds of Realist novel, and different authors use the conventions of Realism flexibly to achieve a variety

of different effects.[1] Nevertheless, one can identify in the practice
of the Realists similarities of technique born of the desire to give a
convincing and faithful account of reality as they saw it. To achieve
this aim the Realist deploys a range of stratagems designed to
enhance the authenticity of what he is portraying. Nothing artificial,
implausible or exceptional which might undermine verisimilitude is
allowed to intrude into the novel. The author keeps himself as much
out of sight as possible to reinforce the illusion that the characters
and events described have an existence independent of the mind
that created them. In practice, the Realists are mainly concerned
with mirroring social reality which they try to represent as fully and
as comprehensively as possible. They range over a broad spectrum
of society, though they tend to concentrate on one or a few individuals. The Realist novel is often a kind of fictional biography, in
which the individual's life is seen in relation to the social and historical circumstances which may be said to shape it. To convey a sense
of the substantiality of the real world, considerable attention is paid
to physical detail in the description of people and places and to
providing the characters with a recognisable environment and
identifiable framework of social contacts. Time is an important
element in Realist fiction, for it is the medium in which people
and circumstances develop and change, and is related to causality.
The Realists believed the world to be governed by a pattern of
cause and effect, whether physical, psychological or historical.
The fact is that the Realists saw the world in a particular way and
the twentieth-century novelists disagreed with them in the first
place not on the fundamental principle that the novel should imitate
reality but on the model of reality imitated. The scientific theories
underlying Realism had largely been superseded by the turn of the
century and new forms of expression were required to fit new conceptions of man and the universe. For one thing, reality was no
longer held to be stable and objectively knowable and writers such
as Pérez de Ayala sought in their novels to fragment reality and show
it from as many different angles as possible. This technique, known
as perspectivism, is the literary equivalent of the theory of relativity.

---

[1] A good idea of the varieties of Realism can be obtained from *The Monster
in the Mirror: Studies in Nineteenth-Century Realism*, edited by D.A.Williams
(Oxford, 1978), which offers a close analysis of a wide range of novels
drawn from different national literatures.

We find, then, that many writers whose work bears little relation to nineteenth-century Realism claim to be offering a true picture of reality as they see it and, indeed, that this picture is more real than the flat, surface realism of their predecessors.

In general terms one could say that the novel turns away from external reality and directs its attention inward. This inward movement manifests itself in two ways, as an exploration of the artist's own consciousness, and as a self-analytical questioning of the nature of the fictional world itself. The two processes are of course related. The existence of external reality outside consciousness cannot be verified and therefore the novel's validity is limited to its own existence as the creation of an individual artist. It can only be concerned with its own reality as art. Fiction becomes the subjective vision of consciousness. This introversion leads inevitably to an increased concern with form as opposed to content, with inner patterns of language, with aesthetic wholeness, with arrangements of motifs and images, with structure and design. At the same time, however, as art diverges from reality there arises a preoccupation with the relationship between the two, between the created reality of a novel and the objective reality of the real world. There has of course always been a tension between the novel's propensity to realism—with its acceptance of the categories of space and time, its insistence on empirical facts, its referential use of language—and the fact that it is ultimately an artful illusion, but modern writers have felt a compulsion to exploit and highlight this tension to an extreme degree. Whereas the Realist sought to disguise the fact that the novel's reality is an illusion, the modern writer seeks to call attention to its essential illusoriness, its artificiality. The subject of many novels becomes the act of novel-writing itself as the author seeks to show himself to the reader in the act of creating.

There emerge, I think, from what I have described, two distinct and opposing views of fiction. On the one hand stands the view that the novel should imitate life, that it should be representative, mimetic. Against this stands the view that the novel as art is autonomous, that it has its own logic and its own laws and is justified by its own inner coherence. No one would deny that Ayala belongs decisively to the new wave of Spanish and European novelists, but it seems to me that his fiction is characterised by a curious ambivalence between these two narrative modes and that nowhere is this more clearly seen than in *Tigre Juan* and *El curandero de su honra*. Ayala's last novel is poised between the mimetic and the aesthetic poles of fiction.

Such a duality in Ayala's approach to fiction is not really surprising for it corresponds to a more general tendency on his part to see things in terms of opposites which ultimately require to be reconciled. Ayala makes the novel assume the function of holding together all the chaos of experience, and claims for the artist the responsibility of discovering the hidden pattern underlying reality. Novelists are 'intérpretes, aunque falibles, de un presunto plan providente que rige los destinos humanos; vates, o zahoríes de la armonía universal' (IV, 946). The writer is a secular priest who reveals truths and values to which his vision gives access. It would appear, however, that as far as fiction was concerned, a form adequate to this religious mission proved elusive, for Ayala abandoned his career as a novelist at the age of forty-five, even though he lived until his eighty-second year. There were personal as well as literary reasons for this silence, of course, as Andrés Amorós makes clear (*2*, 387-96). Ayala undoubtedly found it difficult to get down to serious creative writing. The late twenties and early thirties were extremely busy periods for him. He became very active politically, forming, along with Gregorio Marañón and José Ortega y Gasset, the 'Agrupación al servicio de la República'; he was elected deputy for Asturias, became Director of the Museo del Prado and Spanish Ambassador in London. Then with the collapse of the Republic came years of exile, first in France and then in Argentina. This difficult period, involving long separations from his family and worrying economic problems, ended with his definitive return to Spain in 1954. By this time, Ayala was an old man, rarely venturing outdoors, lacking in will-power and certainly with no incentive to write new novels. Indeed it is doubtful whether, in the Franco era, he could have written the type of novel on which his fame now rests.

This explanation is plausible enough but it does not completely account for Ayala's renunciation of novel-writing in particular. After all, he did continue to write numerous essays and even composed some verse until the last years of his life. There is no doubt that he was discouraged by adverse reaction to his work for, although he has been acclaimed by scholars and serious critics, he never attained popular success. His formidable intellect, his solid erudition and philosophical bent, which found expression in an elegant, polished and slightly archaic style, made him something of an anomaly among his contemporaries and earned him the reputation of being a difficult author. It is true that Ayala's vision of the world is both personal and complex and that his novels can appear strange and puzzling worlds which at times have the effect of mystifying and disconcerting the reader. He once wrote that 'Los libros son despertadores de la conciencia' (IV, 948), by which I take him to mean that man goes through the world looking at things with the eyes of habit so that awareness is dulled. Art helps man regain awareness and enables him to 'ver las cosas como por primera vez, cuando despuntan y van formándose en su luminosa originalidad' (III, 564). By making access to the fictional world difficult, the act of perception is prolonged and things are made to appear unfamiliar. Reality in the novel is not simply recognised but seen in a fresh and unexpected way. Each novel by Ayala is an attempt to extend the limits of the genre by endowing it with new and unforeseen potentialities. Yet for all his attempts at innovation and experimentation he seemed to sense inherent limitations in the form which could not be overcome. He called this, in *Belarmino y Apolonio* (1921), 'la maldición originaria del novelista' (IV, 34). The novelist cannot imitate reality directly, he can only represent it in words, describe it. Already the three-dimensionality of the world is lost. Moreover the novel is a temporal art and narration, being sequential in time, like reading, cannot adequately render synchronicity. It cannot present simultaneous actions and experiences. The novel's very medium, prose, is also the medium of ordinary, non-literary discourse. Being functional and referential, it undermines the novel's aspiration to be an art-form. There is a contradiction here at the very heart of the art of fiction. To Ayala, dealing with shapeless contingency and creating something of formal beauty seemed irreconcilable pursuits; giving an adequate account of human experience while offering an image of an order and perfection beyond haphazard reality and at the same time avoiding the appearance of contrivance proved a difficult undertaking. This is the fundamental irony inherent in Ayala's practice of fiction. A novel must be a whole vision, the imposition of order upon chaos, a means of subsuming contingency into form through the power of art, yet the whole enterprise could be regarded as nothing more than the mind's fanciful fabrication, an elaborate and elegant deceit. Whatever the contradictions in his novels, however, Ayala maintained that art bridges the gulf between consciousness and the world: 'Por el conocimiento estético vamos tomando posesión del mundo exterior y de nuestro mundo interior, mediante nuevas formas' (III, 565). Whatever his apparent theme, then, Ayala is a supremely self-conscious artist pondering the very meaning of the creative act, the role of art in interpreting the world, the nature and significance of literary experience.

As one might expect, this self-analytical presentation in fiction and the concern with design and pattern bear the hallmarks of the poet rather than novelist, and it is a fact that Ayala would have wished to be considered a poet above all. His first important publication to attract the serious attention of other writers was a book of verse, *La paz del sendero*, which appeared in 1903. Two others followed, *El sendero innumerable* (1916) and *El sendero andante* (1921, but written some four or five years earlier). A final collection, *El sendero ardiente*, was published posthumously. Ayala's three short novels published in 1916, *Prometeo*, *Luz de domingo*, *La caída de los Limones*, are subtitled 'Novelas poemáticas de la vida española'. In an interview with Jorge Mañach, Ayala states that all his novels, even those not specifically presented as such, are poematic to some degree.[2] These short novels are poematic in the first instance through the use of poems at the beginning of each chapter which are intended to summarise and crystallise the essence of what is developed in narrative form. Elsewhere, Ayala has urged the use of poetry to express moments of intense psychic experience, the ineffable mysteries of consciousness, thereby dispensing with long passages of psychological analysis (II, 79).

What emerges most clearly from Ayala's thinking on the language of fiction is his belief in the power of poetry to inject new life into the novel by renovating prose and endowing it with expressive possibilities and a concentrated intensity absent in everyday usage.

[2] *Visitas españolas* (Madrid, 1960), p. 154.

It is through the cross-fertilisation or fusion of novel and poetry that he hopes to create what he called the 'integral novel', a mirror of the totality and complexity of experience:

> todo gran novelista ha sido—aunque no haya escrito versos— un gran poeta lírico, pues la única manera de otorgar vida psíquica a los personajes novelescos no puede ser otra sino exaltarlos, cuando llega el caso, hasta la más alta tensión poética y lírica; esto es, subjetiva. Por decirlo así, el novelista-poeta se enajena y vierte en otros moldes de psicología viva. Este es el milagro del gran novelista-poeta. El poeta, nada más que poeta, canta de continuo el aria de su yo. En el novelista-poeta, en cambio, se verifica la multiplicación del yo. Esta multiplicación del yo es perfectamente compatible con el tipo de novela integral que se propone abarcar la realidad entera; o bien, y viene a ser lo mismo, una zona de realidad externa, de perímetro definido, cerrada sobre sí misma, como un orbe autónomo. Aquí está el toque de la novela, como género literario.[3]

The implications of this quotation for Ayala's view of fiction are wide-ranging. By laying stress on 'vida psíquica' rather than on the presentation of objective reality, he points the way to a novel which will portray mental states, that will show an increased interest in human personality. The world of the psyche is possessed of its own reality, and fiction should be rooted in consciousness which is in itself aesthetic. What is involved here is much more than the consciousness of fictional characters, for the emphasis of Ayala's remarks is on the author's own subjectivity. He once claimed that 'Toda obra de ficción es una autobiografía integral. Toda auto-biografía es una obra de ficción' (IV, 996). It is on his own resources as an artistic consciousness that the writer draws. The twin impera-tives of exploring consciousness and making.the novel more artistic are fused in the notion that the artist creates rather than reproduces reality. In other words, highlighting the author's creative role is one way of demonstrating the workings of consciousness upon reality. Artistic creation is analogous to divine creation: 'Si hay algún arte que deba llevar el nombre de creación, será la novela o el drama,

3 *Principios y finales de la novela*, pp. 24-5.

porque uno y otro son como epítome y trasunto de la gran creación divina' (III, 51). At every point Ayala emphasises the predominance of creativity over observation and claims for the artist the power to transform reality: 'el arte no siempre persigue la verosimilitud. A veces la voluntad del artista se sobrepone a la realidad . . . y deforma y transforma las formas naturales.' The novel is made more artistic by the conscious stylisation of the characters, by the creation of parallels and symmetries, by a more poetic use of language, all of which will create a different order of reality, 'una realidad superior, imaginativa, de la cual participamos con las facultades más altas del espíritu, sin exigir el parangón con la realidad que haya podido servirle de modelo o inspiración' (III, 189). The world of the novel will be autonomous, self-sufficient, complex and complete within itself. However, although the whole thrust of Ayala's thinking on art points to a loss of realism in the pursuit of form, he will not sever the links with reality completely. In a characteristic dualism, he sees the created work comprising both art and life: 'Toda obra de arte es un trozo de realidad verdadera en donde están resumidas totalmente, y como en epítome, dos altas realidades: Vida y Arte. Toda obra de arte genuino es condensación de realidades múltiples, forma somera y adamantina donde se compendian formas innume-rables' (III, 42). For Ayala, then, fiction is poised between the order of the world and the order of art. To give a complete account of reality, and human experience of reality, the artist must take every-thing and reshape it in a new synthesis: 'Presentemos la realidad tal cual es, si bien con luz más viva, luz que mana de la síntesis artística' (III, 29). Artistic perfection is the central illumination offering that illusion of completeness beyond ordinary experience, the very experience which provides art's many facets.

Poetry, then, appears as one way of apprehending the flux and chaos of reality, creativity a means of integrating experience. It is clear that Ayala saw the two processes of creating and knowing as in some way related. Not surprisingly, his novels frequently have as their theme the nature of knowledge, the role of the intellect, the power of ideas. Ayala was an avid reader and, although well-versed in the classics, he immersed himself more in philosophical than in imaginative literature. The largest part of his literary pro-duction is in the form of essays, the most important of which are

Las máscaras, published in two volumes in 1917 and 1919 respectively, which bring together his theatrical criticism but also contain
important pronouncements on the nature of art in general. In more
recent years, and especially since the author's death, many essays
hitherto scattered in the pages of reviews and journals have been
collected into volumes. A fondness for ideas, for abstraction, characterises and influences the type of fiction he wrote, and Francisco
Agustín was able to extract a considerable number of essays from
his novels and publish them, independently and unaltered, in a
separate volume.[4] Ayala himself described his particular brand of
fiction as 'un tipo de novela intelectual con ensayos'.[5] The duality
implied by the term 'novela-ensayo' corresponds to a fundamental
principle of Ayala's aesthetics: the reader is required to be both
inside and outside the fictional experience, both to involve himself
in and detach himself from the characters and their situations.
This double response, which Ayala has described as being that of
both actor and spectator at the same time, requires specific techniques for its achievement. The philosophical digression, the superior
vantage-point of intellectual contemplation, the generalised commentary on the action, all provide a degree of detachment which off-
sets any emotional identification. In fact, as I observed earlier, the
use of the dual, or even multiple, perspective is a characteristic
feature of Ayala's approach to reality in fiction. Things are seen
from several different angles, opinions are contrasted, theories
opposed, so that any single perspective is shown to be inadequate,
offering only a partial truth. An absolute truth is the totality of
all possible perspectives, just as a complete work of art is a compendium of many different forms. In everyday life the total view
is not possible but art, by creating an amalgam of unlikely and
disparate components and holding them together in equilibrium,
offers a model or illusion of absolute reality. Underlying Ayala's
aesthetics, then, is a philosophical position.

Ayala has always maintained that philosophical thought is an
essential part of literature: 'Todo arte literario que con dignidad
lleve tal nombre ha de ser en alguna manera filosofía, conciencia

---

[4]   *El libro de Ruth* (Madrid, 1928).

[5]   Interview with Julio Trenas in *Indice*, 116-17 (Sept.-Oct. 1958), p. 5.

esencial de la vida' (II, 560), and he attacks any division of works of
literature into true or false, realistic or unrealistic, on the simple
criterion of whether they examine man from a physical or spiritual
viewpoint. The intellectual tendency manifests itself in prolonged
discussion of ideas and themes in which opinions of apparently
equal validity are opposed and contrasted both to show the limitations of reason and to display complexity and multiplicity as essential characteristics of reality. The weaving of essays into the fabric
of fiction is consistent with Ayala's desire to extend the formal
limits of the novel. When writing of the essays he incorporates
into his fiction, he said: 'En estos ensayos siempre suelo poner
un latido dramático.'[6] This dramatic quality is particularly evident
in *Tigre Juan* and *El curandero de su honra*, of which Domingo
Pérez Minik wrote: 'Siempre nos sentimos ante esta novela como
si estuviéramos en una primera fila de butacas.'[7]

Ayala was an influential drama critic, famous for his contro-
versial criticism of the theatre of Benavente, instrumental in establishing the reputation of Carlos Arniches, and there exists some
evidence that in his early years he wrote and adapted plays.[8] *Tigre
Juan* and *El curandero de su honra* was adapted for the theatre in
1928 by Julio de Hoyos, and the stage version of Ayala's second
novel, *A.M.D.G.*, was performed, amid great controversy, in the
Teatro Beatriz in Madrid in 1931. The ease with which Ayala's
novels have been translated into plays is due no doubt to the predominance of dialogue over action, and to the small number of
characters they contain. On occasions Ayala has recourse to a
play format with stage directions and assigned parts and even when
this is not the case the action is advanced through the conflict of
opinions and ideas. Dramatic presentation furthers the aims of
the 'novela-ensayo'. A novel may be composed in the form of
scenes or tableaux following the pattern of exposition, compli-
cation, denouement, as is the case with *Tigre Juan* and *El curandero*

6   Interview with Julio Trenas in *Indice.*

7   *Novelistas españoles de los siglos XIX y XX* (Madrid, 1957), p. 169.

8   Several critics refer to this. See, for example, J. García Mercadal's introduction to the *Obras completas*, I (Madrid, 1964), p. li; Sebastián Miranda,
'Recuerdos de mi amistad con Valle-Inclán', *Cuadernos Hispanoamericanos*,
199-200 (1966), 6-7; Constantino Suárez, *Escritores y artistas asturianos*,
VI (Oviedo, 1957), p. 137.

de su honra. The use of theatrical devices such as the mask, the *deus ex machina*, the chorus, show up the novel as an illusion, a spectacle, a made-up thing. Ayala actually refers to 'Los personajes de la tragicomedia de Tigre Juan y Curandero de su honra' (IV, 771) and to 'la anagnórisis de suicidio' (IV, 772) in a way calculated to undermine any illusion of reality the novel may have created. The reader is cast in the role of spectator. After all, *Tigre Juan* and *El curandero de su honra* are modern fictional versions of *El burlador de Sevilla* and *El médico de su honra*, or at least are directly inspired by them. The characters are aware of their own theatrical antecedents and almost seem to take part in their own creation. A novel could hardly be more introverted or self-conscious.

This central feature of Ayala's creative instinct, the imitation or adaptation of an existing literary model, is what most robs his fiction of actuality, what most lifts it out of the localising influence of time and place. The important questions are the eternal ones: 'Los grandes escritores son aquellos que mejor han sabido responder a las preguntas esenciales y eternas, según el modo y expresión de su tiempo y pueblo' (III, 209). Ayala's belief in the legacy of the past, in the continuity of human culture, in the identity of man throughout the ages, is reflected in his implicit acceptance of the existence of basic literary structures common to all ages. True art must be in contact with its archetypal roots, for originality, claims Ayala, means precisely drawing on our literary heritage, returning to the age-old sources and patterns of creative inspiration: 'El autor es más original—y no hay paradoja—cuanto más remotas son las resonancias que en él se encuentran; como si dijéramos que sus raíces beben la sustancia de las tradiciones literarias primordiales' (III, 161). The modern novel is set in the eternal context of art, and explores its own reality as art. The self-conscious re-creation of a work of literature in a modern idiom is an acknowledgement of the fascination fictions hold for man. But the device has an important aesthetic consequence. If the reader knows the original work, his attention will be diverted away from, say, character and situation towards an interest in whether the original will be altered or destroyed. He will be looking for the completion of a pattern.

This sense of a completed pattern differentiates Ayala from much of early twentieth-century fiction, characterised above all by its openness, its essential ambiguity, its sense of leaving things unresolved. The great nineteenth-century novels are closed forms, coming to an end either through marriage or death, as is the case in the masterpiece of Spanish Realism, Pérez Galdós's *Fortunata y Jacinta* (1886-7). By contrast, in Unamuno's *Niebla* (1914), the death of the character has precisely the opposite effect, that of opening up the issues the novel raises. Ayala's novels decidedly end with all the main issues resolved, usually in an optimistic manner, for they have the flavour of the fairy-tale happy ending. Ayala exploits the differences between the laws of the world and the potentialities of art and makes literature provide ideal solutions which are absent in reality. Such denouements bring pleasure, but they are rarely convincing. Fictions make sense of experience, but only on their own terms, as fairy-tales, myths or fables. While many artists accept the contingency of the world, and reflect it in novels by finding and developing techniques which will render the arbitrariness and purposelessness of existence, Ayala uses art to give order and shape to the chaos of experience. Using the patterns of earlier literature is one way of imparting form to a novel, of stressing the sameness and permanence of man's way of looking at the world. Borrowed form brings unity into diversity. In *Más divagaciones literarias*, Ayala wrote: 'El problema doble, ínsito a la obra de arte, lo había denunciado ya Platón: desentrañar lo uno en lo múltiple y la continuidad en el cambio' (IV, 1125).

In the preceding pages I have tried to describe the ways in which Ayala deviates from the classic, Realist, mode of fiction. His work is in some senses innovatory and experimental, as we shall see when we come to examine the structure of *Tigre Juan* and *El curandero de su honra*. He is concerned with the artist's consciousness rather than with objective reality. In an attempt to avoid a purely linear or causal development of his plot, he has recourse to a more aesthetic ordering of his narrative through allusion to other works of literature, a musical arrangement with themes and variations, a repetition of motifs, symbols and concepts. But it would be wrong to over-emphasise Ayala's originality. Plot, setting, and especially character find their place in his novels, though they take on a configuration related to the whole fictional experience. While Ayala's approach is infinitely more complex than any surface Realism or deterministic Naturalism, his debt to the previous fictional tradition is obvious. The Realist saw the world, and this really meant society, as stable and subject to verifiable laws that could be accurately reproduced in fiction. By exploring human beings, their actions and relationships, within a set of identifiable determining social factors, the Realist writer hoped to guide his reader towards a moral evaluation of these. At its most basic, Ayala's novel is not fundamentally different. Its central theme, marital infidelity, is common to many Realist novels. The theme is viewed from a social standpoint, but at the same time it takes on layers of significance that transcend the merely social. The novel is composed of two worlds, one real, one mythical. The story of marital dishonour accumulates layers of significance provided by symbolic associations drawn from within the character's own experience, from mankind's deepest archetypal instincts, and from the religious and literary symbols of human culture. On one level, the novel is a drama of recognition worked out through a web of personal relationships and specific social codes. The first part, *Tigre Juan*, is a powerful study of repression, whereas the second part, *El curandero de su honra*, traces an evolution towards a more integrated psychological state. The novel becomes a process of discovery. On another level, this process is represented in archetypal terms as a journey or quest. The social code is made known through its literary manifestations. In the character of Tigre Juan, Ayala creates the embodiment, and then the rejection, of the Calderonian husband, so that as well as dealing with a real and human dilemma, the novel explores the implications of the two best-known Spanish myths, 'donjuanismo' and 'pundonor'. The real and the literary merge and their interaction is central in the final resolution of the novel. The protagonist's psychological integration is explained and paralleled in the artistic integration of the fiction itself.

Such perfect integration, which has led Julio Matas to assert that *Tigre Juan* and *El curandero de su honra* form 'un complejo cuerpo simbólico donde apenas surge un resquicio, abertura o cabo suelto' (*6*, 188), makes the processs of dissecting it through critical analysis seem the very negation of its reality as a fictional whole.[9]

---

[9] In my article 'Myth and Mimesis: The Artistic Integrity of Pérez de

The structure of the novel is meaningful only in terms of the development of the main protagonist, whose psychology is unfolded through a use of symbols, some of which have their origin in old Asturian customs. The mythical or archetypal levels in the work are inseparable from its *costumbrista* realism, just as the treatment of the main character is inseparable from Ayala's exploration of the myth of Don Juan and the honour theme. In all cases, the main integrative element is character which imposes itself as the centre of gravity of all discussion. Critical discussion of Realist fiction has relied heavily on the categories of character, setting and plot. Now that our critical vocabulary has been enriched with a new terminology—narrative distance, point of view, centre of consciousness, foregrounding, rhythm and so on—it would appear almost naive to approach a twentieth-century novel through characterisation. Yet it is an undeniable fact that *Tigre Juan* and *El curandero de su honra* depends largely for its success on the portrayal of a memorable character, behind whom stands a group of minor characters, like him a paradoxical blend of symbolic and life-like qualities. It is this complex treatment of character, I feel, which situates the novel precariously in that indeterminate space between the formless contingency of human life and the aesthetically ordered world of art.

Ayala's *Tigre Juan* and *El curandero de su honra*', *Hispanic Review*, XLVIII (1980), 15-36, I have tried to show how the various parts of the narrative are related. I am grateful to the Editor of *Hispanic Review* for allowing me to use material from this article in the present study.

II *Two Myths:* donjuanismo *and* pundonor

The critic Northrop Frye observes that 'There's nothing new in literature that isn't the old reshaped',[1] implying that literature is made, not of life, but of existing literature. In writing *Tigre Juan* and *El curandero de su honra*, Ayala returns to the *comedia* of Spain's Golden Age, in particular to Tirso de Molina's *El burlador de Sevilla* and Calderón's *El médico de su honra*. The distinctiveness of this aspect of Ayala's work lies in his linking of the archetypal figure of Don Juan to the honour code, in his comic and irreverent treatment of the two themes, which the parodic title of the second part of the novel foreshadows, and finally in his original interpretation of Don Juan himself. Both myths, *donjuanismo* and *pundonor*, have profound social and psychological implications so that Ayala, as well as having a literary aim, is concerned with the role and position of woman in society, especially Spanish society, and with the wider phenomenon of human sexual attraction.

The reasons why Ayala should have wished to base his novel on existing literary myths are cultural, artistic and ideological. In the first place, he seemed to believe in the existence of certain basic impulses and images in man which we could call archetypal and that these manifest themselves in literature as myths, universally recognised expressions of collective beliefs. The incorporation of these myths into a new work is an acknowledgement of cultural and indeed psychological predispositions common to all mankind. Allied to this is the fact that myths are stories which have stood the test of time because of their universal appeal. From a technical point of view, the availability of well-known material provides a short-cut to plot unfolding. The reader is given the pleasure both of familiarity and of novelty for he is offered something immediately recognisable yet transformed by a new context. The borrowed form has a prefigurative function for it directs the reader forward to the completion of a pattern. Its appeal is aesthetic. The juxtaposition of two

[1] *The Educated Imagination* (Bloomington, 1964), p. 28.

modes, however, creates a certain incongruity of anachronism, for each seems to mock the other. At a simple level, the author may use his mythical material to provide a symbolic comment on the events of the narrative, or the reader may be aware of the tensions between the values of the author and those implied in the borrowed model. But in fact there is a curious osmosis in that the ordinary is endowed with archetypal significance while the mythical is contaminated by contact with the mundane. In Ayala's novel, traditional concepts and archetypal literary figures are demythified, while the modern story of love triumphant acquires something of the stature of a new myth.

The myth of Don Juan Tenorio, though typically Spanish, is of course universal. Since his first appearance in *El burlador de Sevilla*, Don Juan has fired the imagination of many different writers including Molière, Byron, Shaw, and Zorrilla, who wrote the best-known Spanish version. In Spain, in the early part of the twentieth century, he attracted the attention of several famous writers including Marañón, Ortega y Gasset, and Azorín, as well as Pérez de Ayala himself. Although we know that the 'convidado de piedra' element in Tirso's play comes from folklore, and Don Juan's motto, 'tan largo me lo fiáis', has been traced to popular tradition, there are no known sources for Don Juan himself. *El burlador de Sevilla*, therefore, seems to have been the original that established the basic characteristics of the myth for others who followed. In Tirso's play, Don Juan is highly mobile, hurrying from one conquest to the next, a supreme actor, undoubtedly promiscuous, unscrupulous and deceitful. He seduces several women, of different social classes, kills the father of one of them and then invites his memorial statue to dinner. The statue returns the invitation and finally carries Don Juan away to Hell. Thus Tirso's play is about divine retribution.[2] Whereas the popular image of Don Juan has rested more on his fame as a great lover, in Tirso's play he is characterised as a 'burlador', who flouts the honour code: 'el mayor/gusto que en mí puede haber/ es burlar una mujer/y dejalla sin honor' (Act II, ll. 313-15). Ayala's version of the myth is therefore faithful to the original in seeing the interrelatedness of Don Juan's exploits and the honour code.

[2] For a fuller treatment of this play see the Critical Guide by Daniel Rogers in this series.

Broadly speaking, *honor* is one of the great motifs of Golden Age drama, first used by Torres Naharro, and is frequently the main theme of the *comedia*. Honour is a social code which supposedly protects the integrity of society and, at its most basic level, means the opinion others have of one. Honour is usually associated with noble status and derives directly from that status. A peasant, then, would not have honour in this sense, only in the wider sense of natural human dignity. Anything that might lower one's esteem in the eyes of others is an affront to one's honour and must be avenged. The dramatic possibilities of such a code are obvious and were most fully exploited in the realm of sexual relations. Though the honour code is encountered mainly in literary form, it has an undoubted basis in social reality. Murder for adultery has generally been seen as distinct from other kinds of murder, particularly so in Mediterranean countries, and it is a fact that at the time when the *comedia* flourished in Spain such murder was actually approved by law.[3] Ayala seemed to sense instinctively that without the honour code, and its insistence on keeping woman protected and secluded, Don Juan could not exist. In his view, an excessive preoccupation with fidelity and virginity leads to a distorted relationship between the sexes. It can culminate in cruel and inhuman acts of violence and encourages immature displays of *machismo*, an aggressive pseudo-manliness which consists in constantly proving oneself to the opposite sex. For Ayala, this unhealthy state of affairs, the product of complex social and cultural factors, impedes the growth of a mature, stable and loving relationship between individuals. It is more likely to produce instability and neurosis, or worse. In his last novel, Ayala undertakes the demythification of Don Juan and of the code of *pundonor*.

Most of the ideas on Don Juan found in *Tigre Juan* and *El curandero de su honra* had been put forward earlier by Ayala in his essays of theatrical criticism, *Las máscaras* (III, 339-90). By analysing Tirso's archetype, Ayala establishes the basic characteristics of the myth. Don Juan is 'hermoso, apuesto y arrojado', 'aunque todavía mozo, ya corrido en años', 'impío', 'mendaz de amor, artimañero' (III, 340). Although basically 'vulgar', he is redeemed

---

[3] See *Honour and Shame. The Values of Mediterranean Society*, edited by J.G. Peristiany (London, 1965).

by a mysterious power of seduction or 'enhechizo' (III, 341). The opposite archetype to Don Juan is Goethe's Werther: 'Don Juan domina al amor. Werther es dominado por el amor' (III, 341), and this distinction forms the basis of Ayala's whole interpretation, for there exists a duality in man's attitude to woman which can be explained in terms of Western cultural history. On the one hand is the chivalrous and Christian attitude of the Middle Ages, the courtly love tradition, which places woman on a pedestal. Woman attracts by her beauty and man must prove himself worthy of her love. Don Juan subverts this order completely by establishing himself as the centre of attraction:'Don Juan no ama, le aman' (III, 341). The Provençal love tradition was a fusion of Christianity and paganism, of spirit and matter, through the agency of Love which, at its highest level, was platonic. Truth, Beauty and Good were indistinguishable, and love was raised to the status of a religion. The cult of Beauty was centred on woman. In Ayala's view this is a predominantly Western outlook, Greco-Roman in origin, and against it stands Don Juan, whose cultural roots are Eastern and Semitic. The rigidity of the Jewish attitude to woman is reproduced in Islam and, because the Moors dominated Spain for centuries, the code of honour and its inevitable by-product, Don Juan, are characteristically Spanish. Don Juan, therefore, represents the coming together of Christian, Semitic and Muslim ideas. Ayala's brief historical survey of attitudes to love and sex reveals how overlaid a natural instinct is with social, cultural and religious significance from which it is impossible to escape.

In *Las máscaras*, Pérez de Ayala takes a largely negative view of the 'tenorio'. Don Juan, in his carnality, lacks the higher senses; he works through deceit and is assisted by darkness. But the central feature of Ayala's interpretation of Don Juan is his questioning of Don Juan's alleged masculinity. For one thing, he has never engendered children. The whole of the Don Juan myth sees the relationship between the sexes as a battle, a struggle for supremacy. Having suspected Don Juan's lack of masculinity and having approached the question in biological rather than purely social terms, Ayala looks to Schopenhauer and Weininger for support for his theories. For Schopenhauer, love is nothing more than sexual attraction, and two individuals are thus attracted when they completely complement each other. In other words there is a process of neutralisation in which masculine and feminine traits reciprocate. In the perfect match there is complete reciprocation (III, 370-1). If this theory is correct, could Don Juan, who satisfies all women, be the *summum* of masculinity? To answer this, Ayala draws on the ideas of Weininger, who begins from Schopenhauer's premises, but argues that no man is completely masculine and no woman completely feminine. Rather each is a mixture of both elements but naturally having a preponderance of one or the other according to sex. Sexual attraction depends on the relative proportions in two individuals being complementary. Woman is completely sexual and is fulfilled in sexual activity. Man is sexual, and something more, and this something produces his higher qualities. The masculine qualities, then, should be cultivated and the feminine left undeveloped. Don Juan devotes himself to satisfying his sexual appetite and must, if Weininger's theory is correct, be more feminine than masculine. This theory of the 'feminoid' Don Juan is exemplified in *Tigre Juan* and *El curandero de su honra* through the character of Vespasiano Cebón, and indeed the very ideas expressed in *Las máscaras* are repeated in the discussions between Juan and his adopted son, Colás. This direct importation of ideas from outside into the narrative is the hallmark of the 'novela-ensayo', with its dual aim of intellectualising experience while converting thought into living drama.

The opening paragraph of *Tigre Juan* is an extended image. The dilapidated buildings of the Market Square in Pilares are seen as a circle of gossiping old hags prying, with malicious delight, into the private lives of others. Ayala offers a grotesque image of public opinion which, when reduced in this way to its most basic and unattractive level, reminds us that the exigencies of the honour code and the common fear of the '¿qué diran?' are different only in degree. Ayala uses ordinary people in ordinary circumstances to undermine the status of the aristocratic code, to make it appear ridiculous and empty. The Calderonian husband becomes a provincial stall-keeper and Don Juan a travelling salesman. In the course of the opening pages of the novel Juan's sensitivity to the question is made apparent through oblique references. He is touchy about any mention, even in jokes, of cuckolded husbands (IV, 554, 559). He is rumoured to have killed his wife when serving in the Philippines, possibly 'como sanción de una ofensa de honor conyugal' (IV, 557), a hypothesis which is confirmed by Juan's forthright views on women: 'La mujer que falta al marido es como soldado que deserta en el frente de la batalla. Entrambos juraron; entrambos perjuros. Juicio sumarísimo y cuatro tiros por la espalda' (IV, 560). This 'fanático del deber y del honor' revels in the role of the Calderonian husband, which he plays for the local amateur theatre group, for in it he finds the literary correlative of his own experience. In a sense, his life is made to conform to a literary model. Ayala explores the theme of the role of literature in people's lives and, at the same time, justifies his own use of a literary parallel. Such justification does little for the novel's credibility, however. A remarkable degree of self-consciousness is required for a character to so detach himself from a novel that he comments on its submerged form, the literary model. The relationship of life to art implied here contains a questioning of the nature and limits of fiction. The character enjoys a measure of autonomy to the extent that he appears to have some part in the process of the novel's making. There is a literary-philosophical dimension to the use of myth which enriches and complicates its social relevance.

On the surface, Juan's views correspond to the Semitic-Muslim conception of woman outlined in *Las máscaras*, and the Christian religion, through its Jewish inheritance, confirms and supports his view of woman as man's perdition, the cause of his banishment from Paradise. It falls to Juan's nephew, Colás, to reject this view. Two sets of values are contrasted in an antithetic dialogue in which the archetypes of Don Juan, 'el vengador ... el segundo redentor de los hombres' (IV, 572), and Werther, 'el fino amador' (IV, 576), are opposed. In this way a state of tension, a climate of equivocation, is created. Ideas are rationalisations of feelings and Juan's and Colás's contrasting opinions can be attributed to their different ages and experience. Colás, young and in love for the first time, is idealistic and in some measure naive. Juan, disillusioned through his own experience, is cynical and embittered. The behaviour of the peasant girls of Traspeñas, of his Captain's wife, Isabel Semprún, and his belief in the guilt of his wife Engracia conspire to destroy any faith he may have had in women. The events of his life and his own inherent nature turn him into a misogynist, with the result that his expectations of women are high and his demands uncompromising: 'En la mujer, obedecer es amar' (IV, 586). Each of the characters, then, is identified with a point of view which conditions their actions. A constant dialectic is maintained: Colás's views seem more reasonable, but Juan's also appear to contain some truth.

As far as Don Juan is concerned, Colás's interpretation is reinforced by his description of the novel's 'tenorio', Vespasiano Cebón: 'con aquellos ojos lánguidos, aquellos labios colorados y húmedos, aquellos muslos gordos y aquel trasero saledizo, no puedo impedir que me parezca algo amaricado . . . tiene anatomía de eunuco' (IV, 577). This description is confirmed by doña Iluminada who singles out his 'facha de mírame y no me toques' (IV, 594) and dismisses him as 'deshonesto y embaucador' (IV, 595). As events unfold, these opinions are put to the test and Juan's trust in and admiration for Vespasiano are shown to be symptoms of his inadequacy with women. Don Juan is the myth to which men misguidedly aspire. Under the strain of emotional pressure, Juan confronts his past for the first time and realises Engracia's innocence and, although his rigid views are not changed, he is made aware of their terrible consequences. An obsession can distort one's perception of reality to the extent that appearances become truth and the innocent are made unjustly to suffer. When Juan falls in love again and decides to marry, he is given a second chance to find a proper relationship with woman, but his insecurity continues to feed his faith in Vespasiano. On learning from him that Isabel is exploiting her daughters for prostitution he reacts in characteristic fashion;' ¡Ah mujeres, mujeres! No sois criaturas de Dios; soislo del Enemigo Malo. Un ángel exterminador, emisario del cielo, habíamos de menester, que os pasase a todos a cuchillo. ¡Bribonas! Pero, a falta de ángel, que sería mucho pedir, satisfágome con un Don Juan de cuando en cuando, como Vespasiano, que os saca de quicio, para luego vengarnos apabullándoos y arrancándoos el antifaz, por donde en vuestra frente se lee: rameras '(IV, 642). The major weakness in Juan's make-up is the manner in which he moves from a particular to a general truth and, indeed, it is impossible to grasp the significance of the literary myth without reference to his total psychology. No man who sees all women as prostitutes can achieve a balanced sexual relationship.

Although Vespasiano himself does not appear in *Tigre Juan,* most of the discussion of the Don Juan figure takes place in that part of the novel. Until his appearance in *El curandero de su honra*, he has existed only in the minds of Juan and Herminia, for each of whom he fulfils a need. Precisely at the point where Juan and Herminia are about to be united, Vespasiano enters the narrative. It is a crucial moment, for Juan is entering a stage of transition from the Muslim to the idealising attitude to woman. Although at the end of *Tigre Juan* he continues to idolise Don Juan (IV, 666), he speaks less of woman in terms of the Biblical serpent (IV, 567) and undergoes a transformation brought about by love: 'Había adoptado altivez y majestad olímpicas. Hacía recordar las estatuas, mayores que el natural, de Júpiter Optimo Máximo' (IV, 671). Norma Urrutia calls attention here to 'el uso de comparaciones simbólicas: la serpiente judaica y los dioses olímpicos. Son el equivalente metafórico de la actitud psicológico-amorosa de Tigre Juan' (*12*, 103). The second part of the novel explores the consequences of Herminia's flight with Vespasiano and, although the Don Juan myth is still present, the honour motif predominates. When Vespasiano eventually makes his appearance, his description (IV, 679) confirms the ambiguous sexuality first noted by Colás (IV, 577) and doña Iluminada (IV, 666). In his encounter with Herminia, he shows himself to be scheming, unscrupulous, insincere and unfeeling, measuring every word and gesture: 'A fin de asegurar el efecto', 'Después de una pausa calculada' (IV, 680), and the full extent of his duplicity is revealed when he uses the very words he had used to Herminia to describe her to Juan. Despite the admiration which Juan professes for Vespasiano, their attitudes and actions are diametrically opposed. Vespasiano's proclamation of free love without commitment or obligation contrasts with Juan's emphasis on duty and honour. In his novel, Ayala, as well as being explicit in his moral evaluation of his characters, also works by a process of analogy. Vespasiano's conception of free love is implicitly contrasted with that of Colás and Carmina, who also contrast with the social view of Tigre Juan. The young lovers are held together by no social bond yet they keep fidelity to one another. Later in the novel, they elope and take to the open road to earn their living 'honradamente', thereby creating a new definition of honour outside the context of traditional social mores and conventional sexual relations. For Juan, this is an affront to 'pundonor' and it is the woman who loses most. For Iluminada, affairs of the heart are personal, above society, and should be oblivious of public opinion: 'La ajena opinión es como la sombra, que siempre sigue al cuerpo, pero por mucho que se alargue o se encoja no la hace mayor ni menor' (IV, 704). What is happening is that Juan, like the reader, is being educated slowly by persuasion and example out of his traditional view. Ayala, by the use of analogy, is working out a series of variations on a single theme, which is multiplied to convey a sense of the variety of human experience of love. Doña Iluminada herself had been faithful to the husband who never slept with her. Outwardly their marriage was conventional and respectable, yet 'No eran hombre y mujer, sino dos socios bien avenidos' (IV, 563). Here a life has been wasted because of an incompatibility that is ridiculous and yet Iluminada achieves a kind of dignity in her refusal to yield to her feelings for Tigre Juan, to her longing for 'otra forma de martirio más emocionante que el sórdido suplicio a que estaba condenada' (IV, 563).

The juxtaposition of Vespasiano's return and the performance of Calderón's *El médico de su honra* emphasises the interrelatedness of the themes of *donjuanismo* and *pundonor*. The production enables Ayala to give a summary of the play and bring out those aspects which have relevance for his novel. Ayala moves away from his technique of treating themes conceptually through the 'novela-ensayo', as he had done in *Tigre Juan*, and begins to explore them more sharply through a reworking of a literary model. Just as Juan's portrayal of Don Gutierre, despite its impact, is undermined by his extravagant costume, so Ayala's twentieth-century version of the Calderonian play is made comic by being enacted in a provincial town by very down-to-earth characters. This is what gives the novel its tragicomic quality. Humour points up the disproportion between the horrible demands of the aristocratic code of honour and the realities of modern provincial life. The wedding ceremony and the failure of Juan, through unfortunate circumstances, to consummate his marriage on his honeymoon, cast a comic light on the whole proceedings which must affect the reader's view of codes which attempt to dignify human behaviour. The interplay between private and public, between personal choice and public constraint, is maintained until the end of the *Presto*.

The *Adagio* of *El curandero de su honra* is built around details borrowed from Calderón's famous play. The situation of Gutierre and Leonor is repeated in the lives of Juan and Engracia for both husbands are deceived by appearances and exact vengeance for an imaginary wrong. Apart from the basic situation, however, Ayala's most important borrowing is the central motif of blood-letting which generates a whole complex of associated images centred on the basic conflict between love and honour which constitutes the main theme of *El médico de su honra*. This conflict is most clearly expressed in the lines 'El amor te adora/el honor te aborrece' which Juan takes up and repeats obsessively in his mind. The use of the double column, which will be analysed in more detail later, enables the honour theme and the myth of Don Juan to be worked out side by side. As Juan reflects on the multiple meanings of honour and reaches a new level of understanding which will form the basis of responsible conduct, Herminia is confronted for the first time with the true image of Vespasiano (IV, 713). The difference between Juan, the would-be Don Juan, and Vespasiano, the real Don Juan, is Juan's capacity for love, his ability and his need to establish a stable relationship with another person. For this reason, Don Juan is condemned to a life of emotional isolation, unable to achieve fulfilment as a human being. As Herminia reaches this conclusion, Juan, in the other column, is beginning to realise just how problematical a concept honour is. As well as a semantic discovery of the many meanings the word contains, practical and ethical questions are raised. If his wife were to deceive him, he should kill her, cleanse his stained honour: 'Lavar tu honor'. But this would not erase his dishonour, which would still remain, and it would also conflict with his feelings. He could kill himself or seek to be blind to the truth. But this would conflict with his duty. Neither course of action would repair his wife's dishonour for she too would have been deceived by her seducer. The answer could be 'Lávala con sangre del burlador' (IV, 714). As Juan weighs up these conflicting possibilities, as he acts out in his mind the literary role, the action is interrupted by a comic interlude, the anecdote of the peasant beating his wife. This sudden switch of perspective provides a humorous and pragmatic approach to marital honour which contrasts with Juan's stereotyped reaction. The peasant chastises his wife, not for infidelity, but for sharing his food with other men. He therefore rejects Juan's view of marriage as possession of woman by man: 'De lo suyo, disponga ella y déselo a quien le parezca' (IV, 716). The implication is that sophisticated social values and conventions are unnatural and at variance with common sense. That the peasant's wife is called Engracia provides the link with the next critical phase in Juan's evolution.

Ayala introduces a new element into the Calderonian situation which significantly alters it. Herminia is expecting a child. When this is revealed to Juan by Iluminada, so great is his emotion that he accidentally cuts himself. The blood image is thereby introduced into a different context: 'Sangre, Sangre. Mi sangre mezclada para siempre con la sangre de Herminia' (IV, 722). The theme of paternity had of course been present from the outset in frequent references to Juan's repressed paternal instincts, and to Colás as a substitute for a real son. The fact that Colás leaves him is his motive for marrying. The sign on his stall had brought together two images, 'sangre' and 'leche', which are now explicitly connected for the first time. Julio Matas refers to these as 'flúidos vitales' and argues that by associating them with Juan at an early stage Ayala invests his character with the important role of helping in the development of future lives (*6*, 174-5). In the honour crisis, the child becomes uppermost, as Herminia explains to Carmen in the brothel (IV, 728) and the thought of it is prominent as she faces Juan for the first time after her return (IV, 749). The presence of a child brings with it new responsibilities. In *Las máscaras* Ayala had written: 'El problema del matrimonio es, en definitiva, el problema de la prole. La libertad individual, el derecho de exaltar la propia personalidad hasta el máximo, con menosprecio de todo reparo, no se pierde en el momento de casarse, sino en el momento de tener un hijo' (III, 307-8). Significantly, before Colás and Carmina have a child, they are married.

Ayala uses all the ritual of St John's Night, traditionally a feast for lovers, to complete Juan's transformation. The motifs of light and darkness, so important in *El médico de su honra*, are reproduced. The bonfires illuminate the darkness. In Sincerato's words 'El Dios de la luz vence al príncipe de las tinieblas' (IV, 726). In a hallucinated state, Juan sees images of Herminia and Engracia who speak to him. He is given a second chance and the multiple associations of blood are evoked. Engracia says: 'Curandero de tu honra, purga tu propia sangre. Purifícate', and Herminia: 'No quiero un hijo de tu sangre. Asesino de mujeres' (IV, 737). In the opposite column, the honour theme is viewed from different perspectives. Iluminada, for a while, upholds the traditional view: 'El cristal, una vez roto, no tiene compostura. Eso es la honra de la mujer: espejo de cristal finísimo, que sólo con el aliento de quien no es su señor legal se quiebra' (IV, 741). An analogy for Juan's and Herminia's situation can be found in the case of Carmen and Lino, who is obsessed with Carmen's loss of virginity. Colás argues ingeniously that such an obsession makes him a prisoner of the past: 'En este país las ideas están viejas, caducas, deterioradas, prostituidas todas ellas. Hasta las ideas de más respetable traza son alcahuetas de algún propósito indecente. Vaya usté con su compañera a un país lejano, de ideas vírgenes, donde el sol de la verdad no sea satélite del negro orbe de la mentira, sino centro de gravitación de las almas. Con la nueva luz verá a su amada como lo que es: un corazón virgen' (IV, 737). There could be no clearer condemnation of a society whose values obstruct human happiness and fulfilment and, just as Lino is able to free himself from adherence to outmoded ideas, Juan is able to turn the traditional concept of honour on its head. Dishonour is brought not by the wife, but by the husband's quest for vengeance. Wife-murder is a greater crime than the offence it is intended to punish. Ayala alters the tragic outcome of Calderón's play: Juan bleeds himself in an attempt to commit suicide, thereby adopting the very attitude he had condemned to Colás earlier. He stops when he realises that Herminia loves him, but the blood-letting is a symbolic purging of his former self. The old Juan has died and a new one is born: 'Don Juan, el Tigre ha muerto. Bien muerto está. Ha renacido otro Don Juan', says Iluminada, to which Juan replies, punningly, that he can be called, 'Juan Cordero, y a mucha honra' (IV, 756).

The novel has effectively ended at this point, but Ayala continues it with the addition of a *Coda*, which serves to show the consolidation of Juan's and Herminia's happiness after the birth of their child, and a *Parergon* which takes the form of a discussion between the principal characters on the major themes of the novel.

In the context of *pundonor* the *Coda* is significant for it portrays Juan as completely indifferent to public opinion. On the train, he confronts Cipriano Mogote, to whom on another occasion he had been uncharacteristically submissive, and who sneeringly implies that Mini is another man's child. Juan's defiance is proof of his new conception of personal honour and there is poetic justice in his making Mogote eat his words. The *Coda* ends with a poem, a hymn to paternity and to the grandeur and mystery of human life. The *Parergon* enables Juan to put forward his views on honour in a calm and considered manner. Although they are similar to his original ideas, the emphasis is on personal dignity rather than on social appearances: '¿Qué es el honor? El honor es la suprema libertad, que no le ha sido concedida nada más que al hombre, y no a las bestias ni a las cosas sin ánima . . El honor es el sentimiento de la propia responsabilidad . . . El honor es fidelidad para con uno mismo. El honor es bravura en arrostrar las consecuencias de los propios actos' (IV, 776). This modification is paralleled by a similar modification of his views on Don Juan. The opportunity for a final comment is provided by the return of Vespasiano. Juan realises that paradoxically he owes a lot to his former friend. Through him and his actions he discovered his true self. By taking Herminia from him, Vespasiano restored her to him. There is no need to punish Don Juan for his perfidy. His actions have a place in the overall scheme of things and, moreover, he is his own victim (IV, 793-4). Juan's double sense of tolerance and justice is reflected in his final ambiguous embrace, part sympathy, part disdain, of this 'deficiente y castrado' Don Juan (IV, 796). He acknowledges that he and Vespasiano are complementary in many ways. Thus the two themes, *donjuanismo* and *pundonor*, are brought together at the end of the novel, having been explored in all their varying facets, their significance and relationship to one another radically re-defined.

Ayala's treatment of the two myths, then, is related to the unifying theme of the novel, the passage from incomprehension to understanding, but of course it raises the whole question of the artistic representation of reality. We can conceive of fiction caught in a debate between history and poetry in the sense that it contains more of the contingent, the accidental, than any other genre and at the same time seeks to justify itself, not only as imitation, but as an art of language. Ayala's use of existing literature heightens our awareness of the artistic qualities of fiction. All of his characters detach themselves, at least momentarily, to discuss some aspect or other of literature. Tigre Juan, clearly, is totally engrossed in the *comedia* to the extent, as Weber observes, 'that real emotional transport can only be compared to the effects of theatrical catharsis, as when he experiences "una manera de dichoso embobamiento, como ante una apoteosis escénica de gran tramoya" ' (*13*, 91). He quotes phrases from *Othello* and *El médico de su honra*, blending together his own lines with those of famous dramatic characters. Colás comments on the story of Werther which enkindles his own nascent romanticism. Doña Mariquita, on the other hand, dismisses works of literature as 'majaderías inventadas para pasar el rato' (IV, 684). Doña Iluminada makes frequent references to fairy-tales and romances of chivalry and seems to see her own role in life as in some way analogous to literary creation. She describes Colás as a 'caballero andante' (IV, 613) or an 'arquetipo de donceles y príncipe de amadores perfectos' (IV, 693). When things go wrong, she describes her part in the tragedy as that of an 'egoísta maese Pedro de este aflictivo retablo, monumento de nubes, tan presto levantado como venido al suelo' (IV, 740), evoking, in Weber's words, 'the classic Cervantine example of the deceptive boundaries between reality and art' (*13*, 94).

This dualism can be seen in Ayala's ambivalent approach to characterisation, for he will not portray his characters as totally realistic nor will he allow them to be regarded as purely fictional. This generates a curious feeling of involvement and detachment on the part of the reader which is an important consequence of making literature out of literature. In short, the author calls attention to his own creative role, to the interplay of subjectivity and objectivity which is characteristic of all fiction. In writing his novel, the author poses the questions: what is imaginative literature and why do we read and write it? The various literary transpositions in *Tigre Juan* and *El curandero de su honra* show the essential fictionality of the work, as the literature of the past acts as a mirror for the new work. As well as *donjuanismo* and *pundonor*, we find a whole series of Golden Age motifs and themes. There are *conceptista* word-plays, puns, the use of the comic anecdote, the intercalated tale, and major themes such as the fugitive and illusory nature of life, and the idea of the world as a dream which is elaborated in the poem of the *Coda*: 'Todo huye y se desvanece./Vivir. Soñar. La vida es sueño./No soñamos los hombres mortales./Nosotros mismos somos un sueño./El mundo es el sueño de Dios' (IV, 770). Therefore, although the novel is a comic deflation of two literary archetypes, its attitude to literature generally is not straightforward. Life and literature are constantly seen to interfere with one another and through conscious manipulation of the narrative, parody and artistic transpositions, the novelist directs attention away from external reality towards the intricacies of the novel's own making.

III Language and Structure

Tigre Juan and *El curandero de su honra* is perhaps Ayala's most conventionally told novel. There is a single omniscient narrator, the action follows a generally linear progression based on causality, and the story is centred on the lives of characters in a specific set of circumstances. But although it is not as experimental or structurally complex as *Belarmino y Apolonio*, the novel possesses features which distinguish it significantly from the traditional pattern of prose fiction. Its most striking structural feature is, I suppose, its division into two parts, each with a separate title. In place of the usual division of the narrative into chapters, Ayala adopts a structure designated by musical terminology, *Adagio* and *Presto* in *Tigre Juan*, *Presto*, *Adagio* and *Coda* in *El curandero de su honra*, in an effort to convey the impression of a symphonic whole in which themes are carefully orchestrated and counterpointed. This principle of organisation creates an alternative structure, free from the exigencies of plot, based on alternations of tone and mood, changes in tempo, effects of antithesis and contrast, the creation of symmetries and parallels, the repetition with variations of key themes. The second part of the novel also contains a *Parergon* and the much-discussed device of the double column. Within each of the main structural divisions, the novel is composed of a series of scenes or tableaux, made up largely of dialogue or interior monologue, which give the novel a markedly dramatic texture.

There is no obvious literary reason why Ayala should have decided to produce his novel in two parts, and its present form may have been accidental. If Joaquín de Entrambasaguas is to be believed, it would appear, quite simply, that the contemporary vogue for books of uniform length made the novel too long for inclusion within a single volume, yet too short for two. Ayala's answer to this problem, which may have been made in response to editorial pressure, was to extend his novel by the addition of a 'documento accesorio' or *Parergon*.[1] If this is so, there is little point in defending the novel

---

[1] Joaquín de Entrambasaguas, *Las mejores novelas contemporáneas*, VII (Barcelona, 1965), p. 337.

as a carefully structured whole. Yet we can assume that the division into two volumes, for which his previous novel, *Luna de miel, luna de hiel* and *Los trabajos de Urbano y Simona*, provides a precedent, would have appealed to Ayala. The addition of the *Parergon* would have seemed natural enough to him, involving as it does the exposition of ideas through dialogue. Given the configuration of the novel as a whole, it is not especially incongruous. As far as the two-part structure is concerned, it is fair to say that, as in the previous novel, there is a difference in quality and emphasis between the two. In *Tigre Juan*, characters and ideas predominate as the basic situation is set out and discussed. In *El curandero de su honra*, the imitation of a literary model takes precedence over any realistic portrayal of the theme. The separate titles highlight differences in technique: the character is seen first in broadly realistic, albeit exaggerated, terms, and then in the context of a literary archetype. Moreover, Ayala had a fundamentally dualistic cast of mind, reflected in the titles of his novels, in his pairing of characters, his creation of effects of contrast, opposition and duplication, all of which reinforce his vision of reality as a co-existence of discordant parts forming an ultimate order and harmony apprehended only by art. This vision has, naturally, consequences for the structure of his novels. The author sees his role as analogous to that of God. It is he who holds the whole of his creation together and is its ultimate justification. By imposing order upon it, by making meaningless experience conform to a superior pattern or design, he provides the reader with an illusion of universal harmony.

Although there is no introductory chapter as such, the opening pages of the novel offer a highly condensed form of exposition in which essential background information is given, the main characters are introduced and the principal themes adumbrated. The absence of chapter divisions emphasises the inseparability of the component parts and facilitates a continuous development of the narrative as Ayala moves easily from description to summary to dialogue. *Tigre Juan* opens with Ayala's description of the Market Place in Pilares whose buildings take on the physical appearance and attributes of those who inhabit it. The description is neither neutral nor objective. It is an extended image in which the narrator distorts what he describes, to convey not the object seen but the impression it gives. Realist concern for detail is replaced by the primacy of the artist's vision. The evocation of an atmosphere of small-town gossip, where there is no dividing line between private and public, alerts the reader to the importance of reputation and the demands of the code of social honour. This central theme is reinforced by the ensuing dialogues between the characters, each of which develops and refines ideas, reveals the inner life of the characters and serves to advance the action. The novel is framed between two opposing conceptions of honour and can be conceived of as a progression, the modification of ideas through conflict, debate and experience. There is a process of destruction and reconstruction as one set of relationships is destroyed and a new and firmer pattern is created. The rearrangement of the pattern of relationships is mirrored in a rearrangement of the structural patterns of the novel. Moreoever, in exploring honour and related concepts through the discursive techniques of the 'novela-ensayo', Ayala underlines the tight connection between language and experience. Words are a form of conditioning which, when charged with social and literary significance, can be a signal for stock or stereotyped responses. In *El Curandero de su honra* Ayala, by using words and concepts as structuring elements in his narrative, highlights the role of language in shaping human behaviour. Language translates reality, certainly, but it also has the power to create reality.

When we talk in terms of fictional language or style we are really using the term 'style' in two senses, style taken to mean those personal idiosyncrasies of an individual writer which recur in all or many of his works and which may be considered as identifying traits, and style in the sense of the particular effects achieved in a work by the use of language which, taken together, constitute the total vision implied by the work. Ayala conceived of the novel as a compendium of styles and regarded the adoption of any one style as a limitation since language and thought are identical. In putting this conception into practice Ayala creates what can only be described as a linguistic patchwork. Thus he moves from the peasant speech of Nachín de Nacha with its reproduction of Asturian dialect: *tolo, güeyo, tabarica, afuxi*, to the language of philosophical debate, to the creation of effects of synaesthesia: auditory and visual impressions merge when la Güeya returns to her kitchen:

'Los vasos ... despedían de sí suaves músicas diáfanas ... los bruñidos cobres de las cacerolas prorrumpieron en unánime grito de luz' (IV, 760-1). But more frequently Ayala's style is expressionistic in that he projects his own attitudes on to the reality described. Sensory functions are interchanged: 'La mirada de Vespasiano era táctil, como si del oscuro agujero de sus pupilas irradiasen elásticos y transparentes tentáculos de molusco, que iban a palpar el objeto con una caricia blanda' (IV, 679). Similarly Tigre Juan feels doña Iluminada's eyes 'acariciándole, como una mano por el lomo de un gato' (IV, 606). Ayala tends to describe mental phenomena in a markedly concrete manner. Colás's ideas fly in all directions through his head like 'los floretes de un asalto'; his imagination is 'como un paisaje montaraz por cuyos riscos brincaban diseminados sus antojos y fantasías, como rebaño de cabras silvestres' (IV, 565). This tendency to substantialise the abstract is an integral part of Ayala's way of seeing reality. Vespasiano's fluency is compared to the dazzling and mesmerising effect of a magician producing objects out of thin air: 'sus palabras producían impresión de abalorios, agremanes, y cintas que le brotasen de la boca como a un prestidigitador de circo' (IV, 679). In fact, there are many occasions when language is made to appear as something solid and words as actual shapes in the mouth. Early in the second part of the novel, the characters listen to the enigmatic words of don Sincerato: 'Doña Mariquita y doña Iluminada, que escuchaban con los labios en hechura de O, murmuraron al tiempo, como si las palabras del cura se les hubieran introducido desprevenidamente en la boca, y luego de paladear la pulpa sustantífica, se apresurasen a expulsar la almendra' (IV, 673-4). An even more extreme case is when the words in Isabel's letter are personified and made to emerge from the page on which they are written: 'Más que palabras eran seres vivos, o resucitados, que se desplegaban, como un regimiento disciplinado, ante Tigre Juan' (IV, 623). These examples reveal Ayala's concern with the expressive possibilities of creative language which is part of his exploration of the relationship between the literary world and the real world. At times his manipulation of language is so extreme that it can become the principle on which a whole scene is constructed. When this occurs the novel asserts its reality as a verbal structure. *Tigre Juan* and *El curandero de su honra* use reality as a starting-point but once that reality is converted into words, language generates a logic of its own which sustains the work through its least realistic phases. Through the power of language, one word leads by association to another, and the novel is justified not by its fidelity to any model of empirical reality but by the inner consistency of its parts.

We can see the importance attributed to the power of language in several ways. Towards the end of the *Adagio*, Juan receives a letter from Isabel, wife of his former officer in the Philippines, which resurrects his past. This is the major turning-point of the *Adagio*. A long flashback to the Philippines explains the origins of Juan's obsessive nature, and the re-enactment of his past has the force of a revelation for both character and reader. Ayala's withholding of this vital information has the effect of binding the reader to the character's experience by a skilful use of chronology. Narrative structure is an analogue of the structure of Juan's experience; the past is kept obscure until it is dramatically actualised in the present. This is no ordinary flashback: it is a dramatic moment in the character's life. From this point on, the structure of the novel is motivated partly by discoveries made by the character. All the action is internal, building up to the final hallucinatory scene in which Juan's consciousness so dominates that the other characters are refracted through his deforming vision to appear as puppets enacting some weird dance of death. The narrative is built around the different meanings of the word 'Apocalipsis', which refers first to the resurrection of the past as Juan returns to his youth and lives again those critical moments of his life. This, in turn, because of its associations of guilt and repentance, is related to the Last Judgement when the bodies of the dead rise again. Finally, this bodily resurrection of the dead is manifest in Engracia's reincarnation in the person of Herminia. A single word, then, generates the complex web of associations with which the *Adagio* ends.

In the *Presto* too words are shown to have a special power. In particular, the dialogue between Iluminada and Herminia contains a play on the word 'querer' which, with its associations of wanting and loving, relates to other words and ideas like free will, marriage, duty. Their conversation moves on to a more lofty plane setting the tone for *El curandero de su honra*. To Iluminada's assertion that she wants for Herminia only what she would want for herself,

Herminia replies:

> Querer para otros lo mismo que para sí es ir contra el querer
> de los demás. Así quieren las personas mayores, que como ya
> no pueden querer porque no pueden conseguir, sólo quieren
> obligar a los otros a que quieran sin querer. Pero los jóvenes no
> queremos así, porque queremos de verdad. ¡Queremos! Eso
> es todo. Queremos para nosotros. No podemos querer sin
> querer ni dejar de querer queriendo. (IV, 659)

A similar display of word-power occurs soon afterwards when the
concepts of truth and illusion, illusion and happiness are contrasted
by the two women. Herminia says: 'A la verdad que me lastima,
prefiero la mentira que me halaga, y con ella me abrazo, porque el
gusto que la mentira me da no es mentira . . . sino que es verdad,
verdad, la única verdad amable' (IV, 661) and, in her own way,
Iluminada concurs: 'Es mentira que la felicidad exista; pero la ilusión
de la felicidad es felicidad verdadera' (IV, 662). The *Presto* has given
the novel a new orientation: argument and discussion have yielded
to a more oracular use of language. Key words, with their hidden
meanings and multiple connotations, reverberate through *El
curandero de su honra*. Moreover, quiet allusions to the world of
fairy-tales point to an archetypal pattern underlying experience
which myths and stories embody. Fictions order experience and help
man to make sense of himself in relation to the world, and the novel
wants to suggest how this is done.

In *El curandero de su honra* the musical arrangement is continued
but reversed, a short *Presto* being followed by a longer *Adagio*,
adding further symmetry to the novel. Until his crisis Juan's life
had been virtually unchanging, static, for twenty years. As if to
emphasise the change, Ayala opens the second part of his novel
with specific remarks on the passage of time emphasising its continuous flux which is experienced rather than measured: 'Pasaron
días, semanas, meses . . . El proceso se verificó insensiblemente,
naturalmente, inexorablemente, sin solución de continuidad. Como
el raudal de un río, iban [los días] resbalando, pues, sin principio
ni fin. Así podía decirse que el día de hoy no era ya el día de ayer;
pero hubiera sido imposible averiguar en qué instante había comen-
zado ni en qué consistía la mudanza' (IV, 671). This indeterminate
period is brought to an end with the fixing of the date for the

wedding for 15 April. This is important for, while we may agree in part with Julio Matas when he asserts that 'Se puede afirmar que el aspecto temporal no es el estructurante de la novela normativa de Ayala' (*6*, 165), the novel has traditionally taken the time dimension seriously. As well as a physical setting, a novel needs a temporal framework. Narration means development in time, a modification of an initial situation. This, in turn, is related to causality: present and future find their origins in past action. Ayala does not interfere with the accepted logic of occurrences in the physical world, though his treatment of time in *Tigre Juan* and *El curandero de su honra* is not straightforward. Towards the end of the *Adagio*, Colás poses questions about how things in the material world change and yet remain the same (IV, 738-9). Such questions are an implicit querying of any one-dimensional conception of time. They suggest a temporal order beyond our ordinary chronological experience. There are moments in the narrative which seem to lift us momentarily outside time. Juan's experience on St John's Night is a case in point. Similarly, when Juan and Herminia come together for the first time after their separation, time seems to stand still: 'El tiempo había detenido también su andadura; si pisaba, era como si no pisase' (IV, 747).

The significance of the encounter is heightened by freezing it in time so that although Ayala does not directly question our chronological experience of time, he implies another temporal dimension. Moments of intense emotion seem to involve an intersection of ordinary time with eternity and through them different orders of reality are linked. A wider temporal dimension is also implied when Juan's and Herminia's lives follow different but parallel paths. The pattern can only be apprehended from the superior vantage-point afforded by art, 'una perspectiva ideal de la imaginación' (IV, 709). This perspective, denied to ordinary experience, is allowed to Juan on St John's Night as he contemplates the whole of reality 'sub specie aeternitatis'. This is, of course, a dimension of time for which the Realist novel has little use, an ultracontinuum in which the novel may be said to exist as an aesthetic object. The reader almost forgets the relation of the words on the page to objects outside the novel as a pattern of internal references is built up. These are apprehended in a way which can only be described as atemporal, suggesting that experience is best understood not in terms of causal explanation and linear sequence but as a pattern of relationships at a given moment.

However, these moments of exceptional experience, though of the essence of the novel, are supported by a series of precise times and dates. This is one way in which the novel approximates to everyday reality. The reference to La gloriosa, the Revolution of 1868 (IV, 599), as part of Juan's youth helps date the novel in the 1890s, as does Colás's departure to fight in the colonies. The whole action of the novel spans just under two years. The action proper begins around October of an unspecified year (IV, 595), the seasons pass until the spring (IV, 671), and Juan's wedding is fixed for 15 April (IV, 672). Vespasiano arrives on 2 April (IV, 677), the day on which *El médico de su honra* is to be performed, and leaves two days later (IV, 685). He returns on 22 June (IV, 705), and Herminia leaves with him the next day. The Capitana had arrived on 11 April (IV, 685), Colás returns at the beginning of May (IV, 693), Herminia gives birth to a son in February (IV, 783). Ayala, then, is precise about dating, particularly in *El curandero de su honra*. There are two flashbacks: Juan's re-enactment of his past life in the Philippines (IV, 623-9) and the *Parergon*. But as well as being realistic in the sense of adhering to the chronology of real life, in order to give authenticity and consistency to the world of the novel, these dates are important in the development of the plot. They reveal a sequence of events which have a profound effect on the principal characters. News of Juan's dark past, apparently confirmed by the arrival of Isabel and her two children, is paradoxically an incentive for Herminia to marry him. Previously, Herminia had been fascinated by his role in *El médico de su honra* in a way which confirms Ayala's earlier psychological aside: 'es propio de la naturaleza femenina inclinarse hacia lo fuera de lo común y perecerse por lo temible y misterioso' (IV, 556). The return of Colás creates special problems for Juan's marriage, as does the return of Vespasiano. Colás acts initially as a bridge between husband and wife but at the same time he encroaches upon their privacy so that Juan is inwardly pleased when he leaves. The departure of Colás and Carmina, in turn, provides a precedent and example for Herminia. The different parts of the novel, then, form interlocking pieces: time is related to causality which affects the psychological development of the characters and adjusts their relationships with one another.

Herminia's escape with Vespasiano takes place, significantly, on the eve of the feast of St John, 23 June. 'La noche de San Juan' is traditionally associated with lovers and Ayala uses all its ritualistic and symbolic associations to endow with archetypal significance the now apparently separate lives of Juan and Herminia. This separation lasts about twenty-four hours and to present it Ayala has recourse, for about thirty pages, to an original division of the narrative into two parallel columns, one narrating the events in Juan's life and the other those in Herminia's. A few pages later there is a much shorter example of the same device. Some critics have felt that what we have here is an attempt on Ayala's part to render synchronicity, for he had complained in *Belarmino y Apolonio* of the impossibility of conveying the effect of simultaneity in narrative: 'ver es como describir con un ojo, paseándolo todo por la superficie de un plano, porque las imágenes son sucesivas en el tiempo, y no se funden, ni se superponen, ni por lo tanto, adquieren profundidad' (IV, 33). For Leon Livingstone, for example, the attempt is 'a brilliant failure'.[2]

In accepting the author's assertion, however, that 'Entre una y otra vida y a través de la distancia era fatal que existiesen mutua correspondencia, misteriosas resonancias, secreta telepatía e influjo recíproco' (IV, 709), which can only be apprehended from 'una perspectiva ideal de la imaginacion', Frances Wyers Weber rightly sees the device as an attempt 'to show, through a series of cross-column and vertical word-plays, the relations, oppositions, counterparts and coincidences between the two lives', and is able to analyse these in detail (*13*, 82-7). Andrés Amorós (*2*, 365) believes that an analysis 'con lupa' would be necessary to reveal these cross-references, but surely Ayala's intention is quite clear. The reader cannot take in the two columns at once. He must read one and when he comes to read the other he will have memories of the first which will affect his reading. Words, phrases and ideas bounce back and forth across the page undermining the inherent consecutiveness of language. The reader perceives the elements of the narrative as juxtaposed at a

[2] Leon Livingstone, 'Interior Duplication and the Problem of Form in the Modern Spanish Novel', *Publications of the Modern Language Association of America*, LXIII (1958), 405.

given moment rather than developing in time.

The first significant word to appear in both columns is 'perder'. Juan uses the word in one sense meaning simply to lose, 'la posibilidad de perder a Herminia', whereas Herminia is thinking of ruin, perdition, 'Caída, perdida estoy para siempre'. Her wilful perdition ('voluntad') through following Vespasiano is taken up in Juan's 'querer es poder' whereupon the two meanings of 'querer' come into play and are linked to 'libertad'. Juan relates the concept of freedom to free-will ('albedrío') while Vespasiano is thinking in terms of free love, which harks back to 'perdición'. Just as Vespasiano gives an openly sexual meaning to 'querer', Juan also thinks of the other meaning of 'perder'. His fears of Herminia's lover's 'blandos halagos' and 'frases deleitosas' are confirmed in the second column by Vespasiano's very words, 'tesoro mío', 'te quiero apasionadamente', 'te deseo con angustia'. The spectre of the deceived husband and the dreadful demands of the honour code now enter Juan's mind but his thoughts are interrupted by a humorous intercalated tale of the peasant beating his wife. This farcical interlude is, as we have seen earlier, a comic variation on the honour theme. The reduction in tension which this sudden switch of perspective achieves is highly characteristic of Ayala's technique, complicating the reader's responses, preventing him from identifying too closely with any grandiose concept of honour, and undermining Juan's tragic potential.

Herminia's pregnancy is revealed discreetly in both columns, through Iluminada's gentle hints to Juan who only slowly realises the truth, and then through Herminia's nausea on the train. The couple are united in parenthood. A new life is about to come into the world as an old life, that of don Sincerato, is about to depart it, thereby creating further symmetry. The high-point of this part of the novel is the activity of St John's Night and is centred on the concepts of blindness and enlightenment. The motif of blindness adumbrated by Juan earlier: 'ciégame, Señor, los ojos del alma y del cuerpo' (IV, 712) is now taken up in the image of light dispelling darkness which, as we have seen, is an important feature of Calderón's play. In succeeding pages the blindness-enlightenment contrast is worked out and given visual representation in the rites of Midsummer. The bonfires blaze in both columns, and both characters experience a moment of illumination, or epiphany, when they become aware of the true nature and meaning of their love. Weber comments that the narrator welds the parallel columns 'into a dense web of inseparable components. Actions, descriptions, and word-plays fit so neatly together that the reader takes a phrase from one column, an image from the other, a scene here, a speech there, and braids the threads into a single chain' (*13*, 84-5). Out of the 'ceguera-claridad' motif, a new theme grows, 'engaño', and the word is explored in all its possible meanings. Colás and Carmina are practising a deception on the people of Mañas (which itself means cunning), while in the opposite column Juan is thinking of Engracia and his own self-deception. He is now hallucinated, his senses deceive him and Engracia's ghost appears to tell him: 'No te engañé. Te engañaste. Te engañaste porque no supiste amarme.' 'Amor' figures prominently in both columns: St John's Night is the feast of lovers and while the others, Carmen and Lino, Carmina and Colás, are united, Juan and Herminia are aware of their solitude. Juan says ' ¡Qué solo me he quedado!' and almost directly opposite in the second column we read: 'Herminia se sentía tan sola.' Reflecting on love, Colás develops the 'engaño' motif: 'La vida está entretejida de sutiles engaños. No hay sino una gran verdad.' But this truth, love, is also an illusion so that the plethora of associations which the word evokes leads to continuous punning and paradox. Juan has undergone a process of 'desengaño', he has seen the light of truth, and is ready to receive the life-giving illusion of love. 'Ilusión' also means happiness. The two principal characters are brought to the same point by a series of intuitive discoveries: 'El diálogo procedía por intuiciones profundas, que sólo se producen en las crisis de tensión emocional' (IV, 736). The parallel course of their experience is revealed in the echoes and cross-references provided by the device of the double column. All that remains now is that they be reunited and this reunion constitutes the final scene of the *Adagio*. Ayala uses the double column again when they are face to face. The parallelism is much more obvious now, for the passage is much shorter and identical sentences are used in both columns while the principle of reverberating echoes is maintained. The pairing of opposites, 'honor'/'deshonra' and 'vergüenza'/'desvergüenza', is used to show Juan's transformation and progression on to a new level of understanding. The *Adagio* concludes with a veritable 'happy ending' but the reconciliation is not the end of the novel. Ayala feels compelled to prolong it with a *Coda* which extends the action until after Mini's birth, and then appends a *Parergon*, which is a flashback to conversations which took place between the reconciliation and Herminia's confinement.

This drawing together of the various strands of the novel is an analogue of the wider integration within the whole of creation, expressed in the poem with which the *Coda* ends. This poem is a hymn to paternity and to life which touches on several themes of the novel as it condenses Juan's 'pensamientos y sentimientos, cada vez más inefables' (IV, 769). Here are woven together images of light and darkness, fire and water, joy and sorrow, to express the mystery and fullness of life. Ayala has extended his novel beyond its logical end to reveal the underlying significance of what has taken place. The events of the narrative alone do not appear sufficient. Plot enjoys a low status in Ayala's order of priorities and the incidents of the novel, contrived as they are in some cases, are subordinate to a general statement on man's position in the world. Nevertheless, the *Coda* appears justified in the context of the novel for in it Juan attains spiritual and psychological plenitude. It offers a confirmation of the stability of his new life in an atmosphere of calm contemplation in the wake of dramatic and overpowering events. It is less easy to justify the inclusion of the *Parergon*, and one is reminded of Ayala's assertion that 'Cuando escribo, imagino hacerlo para los lectores más legos y de más tarda comprensión.'[3] The *Parergon* is the clearest illustration of what is meant by the 'novela-ensayo', the extended discussion on an intellectual level of certain fundamental themes. From a structural point of view, it offers a new perspective on the relationship between Juan and Colás. Their discussions now stand in marked contrast to those earlier in the novel, for their opposing views appear to be complementary rather than antithetical, an impression which is helped by doña Iluminada's role as arbiter.

The novel's structure, then, is controlled by the author's imposition of order and design. On the ideological level, the novel moves forward through the clash of opinions, thesis and antithesis, which are partly resolved in the synthesis of the *Coda* and *Parergon*, as

[3] *Pequeños ensayos* (Madrid, 1963), p. 93.

an atmosphere of conciliation and harmony is made to pervade the final pages. Where there is disagreement, there is an acceptance of the equal validity of all points of view, an affirmation of the relativity of truth. This is the position defended by doña Iluminada: 'Porque exista lo blanco ¿dejará de existir lo negro? Al contrario . . . Lo blanco y lo negro existen y entrambos son verdad. Dejemos a cada cual con su verdad, siempre que sea de buena fe, aunque nuestra verdad sea más noble y más bella' (IV, 779). All hypotheses are unverifiable objectively but useful as a subjective view of reality. The only interpretation of the world which is manifestly false is that which in its partiality claims to be absolutely true. As Juan now recognises: 'los defectos de los hombres . . . tienen por causa haber tomado como total razón de ser de la vida lo que no es más que una parte de ella' (IV, 790). Totality is achieved by the continual merging of opposites, which is what the final embrace of Juan and Vespasiano is meant to signify: 'Meterte dentro de mí y meterme yo dentro de ti. Eres una parte de mí mismo, que me falta; como yo debiera ser parte de ti' (IV, 796). The interplay and final resolution of dualities and antitheses is the most salient feature of the novel's structural pattern, the aesthetic equivalent of another complementary relationship, that of the conscious and the unconscious, in which unconscious forces are seen to collaborate with consciousness by symbolic and artistic means. This relationship is a psychological analogy of universal harmony which encompasses apparent contradictions in a sort of 'acorde discordante' (IV, 688).

Summarising, it seems to me that one can isolate two basic structural principles underlying the novel, one causal or realistic, one aesthetic or artistic, the latter growing out of the former. One could argue that this is the most fundamental duality in the work: it is presented on two levels. On one level, the characters function as real people and their lives are governed by the laws and circumstances of the real world. On another level, they appear as ingredients in a work of art. Tigre Juan, the person, is also 'el curandero de su honra', the literary representation. The central themes of the novel are represented in concrete symbols. Thus a concept like 'illumination', highly relevant in a novel which charts a character's progress from blindness to enlightenment, is embodied in Don Sincerato's school for blind, deaf and dumb children. This acts as an image of man's incapacity to discover the world through his senses and communicate with other people: 'Ojos tienen y no ven; oídos, y no oyen; boca, y no atinan a expresar lo que quieren' (IV, 667). The concept is further explored through the characterisation and name of doña Iluminada and is given its most visual expression in the bonfires which illuminate the darkness on St John's Night. A network of literary echoes and reminiscences relates the character's experience to its most memorable embodiment in literature. Similarly, the author in his handling of time does not renounce sequential arrangement entirely. The action is circumscribed within accepted temporal and spatial categories and it is possible to trace a pattern of causality at work. Nevertheless, the use of literary models gives the novel a timeless mythical content creating a sense in which experience resists the imposition of a strict chronological order. The repetition of the story of Engracia suggests a pattern of eternal recurrence; the freezing of the action into static images implies an escape from the tyranny of time into a kind of abiding present. More simply, the author describes events not in the sequence in which they occur but in a pattern judged to be aesthetically significant. Therefore alongside experience which purports to be real is placed experience which is seen to have been shaped artistically. In creating obvious symmetries, in elaborating concepts through symbols, in manipulating perspective, in surrendering to the power and pleasure of words themselves, the author views his creation with an aesthetic detachment. The novel offers both reality and its artistic representation.

IV Characters and Archetypes

In his prologue to the 1942 edition of *Troteras y danzaderas*, Ayala defined the function of secondary or episodic characters:

> el personaje episódico y el episodio sólo cabe que cumplan en dos funciones esenciales. Una: provocar o estimular en el protagonista reacciones de conciencia, y consecuentemente tal vez de conducta, en una serie de presentes vitales para él. Otra: representar la diversidad de las actitudes fundamentales frente a la vida, enfrentadas por tanto entre sí, con que el personaje episódico pasa a ser, cada cual a su turno y en su presente, personaje principal.

As the titles of both parts of the novel suggest, *Tigre Juan* and *El curandero de su honra* is centred on one character and the principal interest of the work resides in Ayala's complex treatment of him and his psychological evolution. But although Juan predominates, there are ranged around him several secondary characters of varying degrees of importance who give depth and substance to the world of the novel. This broad function, which is a legacy of nineteenth-century Realism, is refined in Ayala's fiction. The number of minor characters is greatly reduced, and they have a more specialised role than merely supplying background. The functions which Ayala mentions in his 1942 prologue are closely related in *Tigre Juan* and *El curandero de su honra*. Each of the main secondary characters—doña Iluminada, Colás, Herminia, Vespasiano—plays a crucial role in Juan's process of self-discovery, while at the same time they represent different attitudes to life based on their own particular 'razón de ser'. This diversity of opinion and experience finds expression in the 'novela-ensayo' for the characters speak more than they act, exploring in their conversations the many facets of truth. It is, therefore, impossible to separate characters and themes in the novel. It is significant that when Ayala talks about characters he talks about 'reacciones de conciencia' and 'actitudes fundamentales frente a la vida'. Characterisation is conceived in such a way that it contributes to the total vision of life implied in the novel's meaning.

The apparent subordination of characters to concepts has occasioned more sustained criticism than any other aspect of Ayala's work.

The very articulateness which Ayala's characters display has given rise to much critical unease, especially when one considers how often it appears inconsistent with their social status and education. Rufino Blanco Fombona has claimed that 'aun los más humildes suelen discurrir como doctores de Salamanca'.[1] Such an objection is only part of a much wider criticism of Ayala's method of characterisation which seems to many to depart too radically from the conventional expectation that characters should be fully delineated individuals, plausible models of the kind of people one might meet in the real world. F.C. Sainz de Robles, for example, complains that Ayala creates 'personajes símbolos, personajes paradigmáticos, de quienes se sirve el novelista, amañadamente, para la oratoria de su filosofía o de su estética'.[2] Juan Chabás agrees and offers a description of how he thinks Ayala set about composing his novels. Firstly, he has a theme or concept which he wishes to explore in narrative form. Then, 'cuando todos estos escolios, cuestiones o teorías llegan a ser en Pérez de Ayala una vivencia literaria intensa, el autor inventa unas figuras humanas que pueden incarnarlos. Al nacer estas criaturas, engendros poéticos o entes de la razón de Ayala, no aparecen dotados de bulto físico muy determinado. No pueden ser, desvalidos de su cuerpo, sino símbolos del tema.'[3] As far as *Tigre Juan* and *El curandero de su honra* is concerned there is some evidence that Ayala worked from living models.

Francisco Agustín is the earliest critic to mention the existence of a real-life 'Curandero de Oviedo' (*1*, 211) and this appears to be confirmed by the evidence of Adolfo Posada who remembers that he was even called Tigre Juan.[4] In an interview with Juan Antonio Cabezas two years before his death Ayala agreed that Tigre Juan did exist but said that he was only the starting-point on which his

---

[1] *Motivos y letras de España* (Madrid, 1930), p. 145.

[2] *La promoción de 'El cuento semanal'* (Madrid, 1975), p. 144.

[3] *Literatura española contemporánea (1898-1950)* (Havana, 1952), p. 277.

[4] 'De mis recuerdos: "El Tigre Juan" o "Don Juan el Tigre" ', in *La Nación* (Buenos Aires), 25 January 1942.

creative imagination went to work: 'Tigre Juan tuvo su tenderete y cuchitril en el mercado del Fontán. Pero sólo me sirvió de trampolín para disparar la fantasía. Lo demás, su pintoresca retórica, su retorcida madeja psicológica, se la metí yo dentro.'[5] In the same interview, Ayala claimed that doña Iluminada was 'pura ficción', though José Zaloña claims to have traced her to a friend of Ayala's father.[6] This evidence, and there are sources for characters in other novels, lends some weight to Ayala's own claim that he does not think in terms of themes or symbols which are subsequently turned into characters for the purpose of a novel. The object, or character, is presented with such intensity that it acquires the force of a symbol. This is the cornerstone of Ayala's creative method: 'Cuando una cosa se nos da con realidad acusada enérgicamente adquiere un valor de símbolo para todas las cosas de la misma especie. Este es el procedimiento más eficaz del simbolismo artístico. El procedimiento inverso de extremar un concepto y luego infundirlo en una individualidad de ficción, me parece, además de falso, peligroso' (III, 84).

There is no incompatibility between creating characters which have some realistic base and endowing them with symbolic significance. Ayala's characterisation combines rich particularity with universality, for his characters exist on several levels at once, realistic, symbolic, literary. Thus Tigre Juan is a small-town homeopath, a symbol of social honour and duty, the embodiment of the Calderonian husband. In other words, Ayala distorts the natural in the interests of the symbolic. If the typical is at times preferred to the individual it is because it appears closer to the essential reality that lurks behind particulars.

Ayala has no reply, however, on the grounds of Realism, to the criticism, voiced by E. Díez-Echarri and J.M. Roca Franquesa, that he tends to 'hacer hablar a sus personajes en un estilo que no les corresponde'.[7] But if one accepts the heightening of reality that Ayala's method involves, then the long, erudite dialogues form

[5] *España semanal* (Tangier), 17 July 1960.

[6] 'Recuerdo ovetense de Pérez de Ayala', *La Nueva España* (Oviedo), 14 August 1962.

[7] *Historia general de la literatura española e hispanoamericana* (Madrid, 1960), p. 1382.

part of that process. The normal method for expressing the deepest thoughts and feelings of not too articulate characters is to use some form of interior monologue. Thoughts are much less determinate than speech so that the essence of what the characters mean is conveyed in words which they themselves would not use. In this way, verisimilitude would be maintained. On occasions Ayala does this, but it is not his general practice. There seem to me to be two reasons for this. In the first place, repeated use of the device would have led to a lessening of dramatic tension and, as we have seen, conflict of ideas is a fundamental principle of the development of the narrative. Secondly, Ayala is not aiming at strict Realism, which ultimately blurs the distinction between literature and reality by forcing literature into the patterns associated with one particular interpretation of reality. Stylised language is one way of raising the character's experience above the merely personal. What is lost in verisimilitude is gained in archetypal intensity. The art of fiction is primarily an art of language. When characters speak 'out of character' they remind us forcibly of this fact.

This is not to say that the characters of the novel all speak in the same style. Quite the reverse, for each has a distinct and individual manner of speech. Nachín de Nacha speaks in Asturian dialect. Tigre Juan varies his style according to the social status and education of his interlocutor. Doña Iluminada's language is largely rhetorical, characterised by word-plays, aphorisms and highly formalised phrasing. Don Sincerato uses short sentences interspersed with Latin and meaningless sounds, a 'surtido repertorio de exclamaciones por aliteración y consonancia' (IV, 633).

To Díez-Echarri and Roca Franquesa's other charge that his novels contain 'demasiado lastre intelectualista' and that as a result they are lacking in human qualities, Ayala replies that there is no incompatibility between the intellectual and the human, for they are both integral parts of experience:

> Hay quien opina que mis personajes son harto intelectuales y raciocinantes, encierran un sentido místico y frisan en el símbolo; de donde resultan poco humanos, poco verdaderos, poco comunes, poco convincentes. Claro que estos calificativos no se compaginan entre sí. Un personaje raciocinante tiene grandes presunciones de ser convincente; cuando menos

aspira a serlo. Lo intelectual no es lo más común, concedo; no se tropieza con un Hamlet a la vuelta de cada esquina. ¿Hemos de negar por eso el carácter de real o verdadero a lo intelectual? En cuanto al mito o al símbolo, si no son manifestaciones esencialmente humanas, ya no sé lo que son. El espíritu de cada hombre, aun el más lego, no se alimenta sino de media docena de mitos y símbolos elementales. (IV, 997-8)

There is therefore a dual conception of character implicit in Ayala's method. Seen from one point of view these are real people enacting very real dramas, seen from another they are symbols or archetypes. Like Ayala's dual treatment of time, his treatment of character reveals the twofold nature of his fictional enterprise, aiming both at some kind of fidelity to experience and at a consciously artistic representation of it. Ayala's angle of vision, then, is never constant and his approach to character is multifarious and complex. He alternates inside and outside views, adopts a sympathetic and then ironic perspective, makes physical descriptions and characters' names provide the clue to their natures and role in the story. A consistent technique is dehumanisation.

Ayala believed that too close identification between reader and fictional character tends to undermine genuine aesthetic experience and that, in order to combat any sentimental involvement, he adopts an intellectual approach to his subject-matter or uses humour to distance the reader from what is taking place. If a character is robbed of his human appearance and attributes, the reader's sympathy is unlikely to be engaged. But Ayala's dehumanising tendencies, as well as serving to create aesthetic distance, seem to be part of an overall vision of existence which sees affinities between persons, animals and animate and inanimate matter, all of which are linked in the evolutionary chain. In *Las máscaras* he refers to this phenomenon:

Todas estas formas vegetales y animales no se presentan autónomas, separadas, distintas, sino envueltas, enredadas; y aun más, entretejidas y en continuidad no interrumpida; de suerte que las vegetales brotan de las minerales, sin emanciparse enteramente de la inercia, y las animales de las vegetales, sin eximirse del todo de la naturaleza vegetativa, estableciendo así una jerarquía de lo inferior a lo superior, de lo más sordo a lo más sensible. (III, 331)

Thus Tigre Juan (IV, 553) and Colás (IV, 565) are described initially in terms of animals and things. Juan's emotions, for example, manifest themselves like chemical reactions. In moments of anger 'la dura cara de cobre se ponía broncínea, verde cardenillo, como si, de súbito, se oxidase con la acidez de los sentimientos' (IV, 554). In a real fury this is intensified: 'Su piel de cobre no era ya amarilla ni verde, sino escarlata, como metal en fusión' (IV, 600). But Ayala's grotesque or dehumanising vision is not usually sustained throughout a work. The main characters in particular are progressively humanised, though to counteract any tendency to sentiment he will introduce a discordant note into a potentially emotional scene. The wedding of Juan and Herminia, which is so charged with significance for Juan, appears almost farcical when viewed from the outside. Juan wears 'la carátula grotesca y los arreos del petimetre', Herminia's feet are compressed into shoes several times too small. To complete the comic scene, the ceremony is attended by twenty-five deaf-mutes: 'Todos eran desmedrados, voluminosa la cabeza, hacían muecas y visajes ridículos como bufones enanos' (IV, 688).

The very minor characters are often the most grotesque. Herminia's grandmother, doña Marica, never appears as an attractive figure: 'Esta vieja era tramposa como otros son zurdos o gangosos: por constitución natural' (IV, 620). To her natural deceit is added a hideous physical appearance (IV, 632). As a sort of identifying trait, Ayala has her eating sweets every time she appears (e.g. IV, 632, 772). Doña Marica is usually found in the company of the old priest, don Sincerato Gamborena who meets Tigre Juan nightly in her house to play cards. He too is made to appear grotesque: 'Era muy bajo de estatura, casi enano; estaba en los puros huesos. Su cabeza era descarnada, manifiesto el cráneo bajo la piel a él adherida, que era charolada y precisamente color de hueso' (IV, 631). Dressed in black with his large top hat dominating his diminutive frame he looks like 'un frasquito de tinta con corcho de botella de litro' (IV, 632). His cough and his laugh contort his face into the masks of tragedy and comedy: 'Diferenciábase la risa, risa de calavera, de la tos, tos macabra, por el trazo que describía la cavidad de la boca, que en la tos era como carátula de la

tragedia y en la risa como máscara de farsa' (IV, 632). He is characterised by his meaningless expressions of infantile delight and excitement. Both these characters, old, bony and ghostlike, figure in Juan's
doomsday vision at the end of the *Adagio* of *Tigre Juan* where in
his hallucinations he sees them as skeletons performing a Dance of
Death on the Day of Judgement (IV, 634-5). The original descriptions of the characters prepare the way for this nightmare vision.
One recurrent feature in the description of Sincerato is the reference
to the mask. Ayala was fascinated by the contrast between the real
self and the false image projected to the outside world. Social relationships involve role-playing. Juan, for example, 'atemperaba su
lenguaje a la inteligencia, estado y estilo del interlocutor. Con las
personas educadas procuraba hablar por lo retórico. Con Nachín
de Nacha, el aldeano, empleaba voces y giros del dialecto popular'
(IV, 559). On other occasions, however, the mask is involuntary,
as when he tries to speak softly to the children: 'Se esforzaba en
susurrar palabras mimosas y dulcificar el acento; pero no le salían
sino expresiones torvas y un rugido bronco' (IV, 558), or with
Carmona: 'Habíase esforzado ahora en componer una sonrisa benig-
na, melificada. A pesar suyo, presentaba una carátula de sayón,
sicario o esbirro, que se refocilaba en el tormento de su víctima'
(IV, 597). The biggest mask of all is Juan's *persona* as the Calderonian
husband: here the mask has a psychological origin as a defence
mechanism. Other characters are more consciously actors. Vespasiano
has a mask to suit any occasion. In his first meeting with Herminia
in the novel he measures every word: 'A fin de asegurar el efecto,
buscó una frase de conmiseración . . .' (IV, 680). Behind this phrase
lurks another of Ayala's theories. For the actor, the maximum
effect is achieved by the minimum of involvement, so Vespasiano
proceeds with coolness and calculation. On the train, 'Con celeri-
dad de estratega amoroso, avezado en celadas, efugios, asaltos y
maniobras de envolvimiento, Vespasiano tendió mentalmente las
líneas maestras de su plan' (IV, 715). Ayala uses military images
to point up his lack of spontaneity and to show Don Juan's love-
making as a conquest or skirmish between the sexes. But Don
Sincerato represents a further refinement of speculation on the
mask. Although grotesque and apparently insignificant, he has the
role of expounding a central theme of the novel: the paradoxical

nature of reality. It is summed up in his words: 'Los que llamáis ciegos son los que mejor ven, porque no han menester luz' (IV, 667), which echoes the motifs of light and darkness which are the metaphorical correlatives of the theme of ignorance and under-standing, the progression from a false, surface view of the world to a true vision, the revelation of the authentic face behind the mask.

Don Sincerato, in contrast to the vast majority of clerics in Ayala's novels, is a good priest and his name is meant to imply this. The simplest form of characterisation is, of course, the significant name though in real life we do not expect any correspondence between a name and a person's character. Ayala does not shy away from the fact that he has the task of naming his characters and takes full advantage of the possibilities open to him. Tigre Juan suggests Juan's fierceness, and the deferential 'don Juan' conjures up the desired side of his personality. The fact that his real name is Juan Guerra Madrigal reveals the duality of the man and the opposition between the two sides of his nature. Ayala is happy to call attention to this 'pareja nada compatible de apellidos que, como perro y gato, sorprende ver juntos y concordes' (IV, 556). The name **Vespasiano Cebón** is highly suggestive. Vespasian, the Roman emperor, suggests decadence, and Cebón implies fatness (cf. 'cebo', 'sebo'), both of which accord with his description: 'Era guapo, con una belleza decadente de emperador romano o de señora madura en libertinajes' (IV, 679). As we have seen, this sexual ambiguity is the aspect of the Don Juan figure which Ayala's novel most accentuates.

Dualities, ambiguities and oppositions, however, are seen not only within characters but between them. Doña Mariquita contrasts with doña Iluminada in her tastes: 'Doña Mariquita era partidaria de un lujo estrafalario y chillón . . . Doña Iluminada defendía la intimidad y la sencillez' (IV, 675). Juan's need for permanence and stability contrasts with Colás's desire for movement and change. Iluminada and Vespasiano represent two opposing kinds of sterility: 'Doña Iluminada representaba una electricidad positiva respecto de Vespasiano, electricidad negativa. Doña Iluminada era la esterilidad desengañada y resignada que, no siendo de provecho para sí, resuelve emplear su energía inútil en beneficio ajeno. Vespasiano era la esterilidad insumisa, que se engaña a sí propia y pretende engañar a los demás, desviviéndose en hacer pasar el libertinaje como exceso genesíaco, derroche de potencia y voluntaria renuncia a la fecundidad' (IV, 676-7). The characters are arranged to contribute to the novel's sense of proportion and balance. Herminia undergoes a parallel process of discovery to that of Tigre Juan. Each has another character, Engracia and Vespasiano, who symbolises their inner conflict. The main couple is duplicated by Colás and Carmina who represent another possibility in male-female relationships, and Lino and Carmen, in turn, offer yet a further perspective on the related themes of love and honour. At the basis of all these situations is the problem created by the conflict between individual feelings and social pressures. Through the analogies between the characters the theme of love is experienced in all its diversity: love as simply carnal or sexual instinct, love as the antithesis of illusion, love experienced as privation, love as existing for others as well as oneself, and so on. Iluminada engineers the love both of Juan and Herminia and of Colás and Carmina. Herminia herself assumes the role of intermediary in the intercalated love-story of Carmen and Lino. So although the characters function to some extent as individuals, they take their place in the overall design and they assume symbolic significance. Juan and Herminia are masculine and feminine archetypes as several lines make clear. Iluminada sees Juan as a 'dechado y arquetipo de cualidades masculinas' (IV, 564) and tells Herminia: 'eres toda una mujer' (IV, 662). Doña Iluminada herself, as well as being a real person full of wisdom born of experience, has a symbolic role in that she is the *deus ex machina* of the tragedy who guides the protagonists to their moment of illumination. Her name is therefore significant. Images of light and darkness surround her every appearance, images, as we have seen, associated with the novel's main theme (cf. IV, 561). This light-darkness duality reflects Iluminada's blend of youth and old age, and the only 'vislumbre de amanecer en la noche perpetua de la viuda' (IV, 564) is her love for Tigre Juan and the hope that it will be returned. She also possesses the qualities of a mind-reader or prophet, for she penetrates Juan's protective shell to discover his true nature and foretell that he will marry again. In fact, there exists a telepathy between Juan and Iluminada for he realises, unknowingly, the secret of her virginity in marriage, a state which is described in terms of quasi-religious concepts such as 'martirio', 'suplicio', 'heroicidad', 'sacrificio' which tend to make her seem more spirit than matter. In fact Iluminada never is really described and remains for the reader, as for Juan, 'desprovista de existencia corpórea, era como un fuego fatuo, ingrávido y vagamente luminoso, temblando en la frontera del más allá' (IV, 579). Later she is described as 'colindante entre el mundo de la materia y el del espíritu' (IV, 582). By detaching herself in part from this world she is able to achieve vicarious pleasure and satisfaction from arranging the happiness of others, a further paradox in the novel: 'Dios me condenó a la esterilidad para ser más fecunda' (IV, 654). She adds to the story-like quality of the novel by appearing as a fairy godmother at the opportune moment. She actually tells Carmina the story of the 'hada madrina', and explains Herminia's situation through the fairy-tale of Beauty and the Beast. In this sense, doña Iluminada is the most literary of all the characters both because of the way Ayala characterises her and because she endeavours to make the events of the novel follow the pattern of a romantic story. Weber calls her 'a kind of assistant novelist' (*13*, 93) who scripts parts for other characters. When things go badly wrong, she blames herself as 'la autora de todo' (IV, 728) or 'la autora de tanta tragedia' (IV, 740). This is a further twist in Ayala's treatment of the relationship between life and literature. He turns reality into fiction; Iluminada makes that reality conform to the models of fiction. At all times, she is a light in the surrounding darkness: 'el óvalo nítido, casto, incorpóreo del rostro de doña Iluminada', 'el rostro de plata lúcida'. As Weber observes: 'The author has given a person a symbolic name and exemplified its diverse connotations in descriptions and in the novel's plot. Iluminada's character emerges from a system of co-ordinated metaphors' (*13*, 35). Yet G.G. Brown can describe her as 'a very real person'.[8] Her sagacity is revealed in her numerous aphorisms particularly on relations between the sexes and in her ability to see beyond the surface of things. She supplements with concrete observation Sincerato's words on the paradoxical nature of reality as, for example, when she gives her views on Juan's fear of women (IV, 564), or on the real value to Juan of Colás's departure (IV,

[8] *A Literary History of Spain: The Twentieth Century* (London, 1972), p. 44.

613), or on Herminia's revulsion from Juan being in reality a desperate defence against attraction. With her 'natural perspicacia' (IV, 640), she offers new views of, and commentary on, the action and along with Sincerato Gamborena and his school of deaf-mutes fulfils the role of chorus.

Nachín de Nacha exists only in relation to Tigre Juan. First introduced as 'el de las monteras, viejo ladino y muy terne' (IV, 558), he provides a link with the world of nature and rustic superstition. He represents a rejection of urban life, and his language is characterised by the use of popular dialect. When Juan experiences real difficulty in accommodating the conflicting demands of emotion and social convention, Nachín de Nacha holds out the temptation to flee to the wilds. His peasant wisdom is hard to resist: 'Tú no compriendes el canto del cuquiello, ni quieres creer en las xanas, el trasgo y el duende, y la huestia y la santa compaña. Fías, en cambio, y crees en los hombres . . . Sombras, na más que sombras, son todos estos hombres y muyeres que nos arrodean' (IV, 610-11). Clearly this is yet another reference to the illusory nature of life pointing to some other reality beyond the immediate. Nachín's references to the superstitions of the countryside and to age-old Asturian customs prepare the way for the ritual and magic of St John's Night, but curiously on that occasion his is the voice of common sense. He provides Juan with his only tenuous link with reality:

> TIGRE JUAN: ¿Qué hijos de mala madre se ríen de mí con burla sigilosa, que se extiende y cubre la tierra?
>
> NACHIN DE NACHA: Son los grillos. Anda pa casa.
>
> TIGRE JUAN: El clarín del arcángel parte por mitad el silencio. Una espada de luz increada rasga el velo del firmamento, como toldo de seda crujiente.
>
> NACHIN DE NACHA: El gallo cantó. Media noche. (IV, 737)

The use of a play format, incidentally, underlines the dramatic nature of Juan's experience and renders his words with more immediacy and intensity. The narrator effaces himself and events are seen as they happen, not narrated. But the device cannot but appear somewhat artificial and thereby become conspicuous. The reader is made conscious of the artistic/theatrical presentation of the material.

Just as Nachín de Nacha has little significance divorced from Tigre Juan, similarly Carmina is dependent on Colás and doña Iluminada for her place in the novel. She first appears in Iluminada's doorway 'una chiquilla como de dieciséis años, harapienta, flaca, morenucha, de grandes ojos radiosos' (IV, 588-9). Her life is completely moulded by Iluminada, who prepares her for the return of Colás, feeding her with romantic literature: 'Carmina leía novelas de viajes y aventuras que doña Iluminada le compraba' (IV, 691). Ayala plays with the orders of fiction and reality, the infinite perspectives of art. Carmina is the literary creation of his creation. She has a function in relation to Juan by showing his fear of expressions of feeling (IV, 590) and by fulfilling for the time the role of idealised woman, a substitute for Herminia, 'símbolo suficiente, por lo visible, de la otra mujer, velada todavía tras el cendal de una nube' (IV, 648). Carmina symbolises young, innocent love and when Colás returns, she responds to him with an 'amalgama de amor apasionado, gratitud y orgullo'. They elope, forming an idyllic picture: 'componiendo una sola sombra ingrávida, color violeta, enlazados por la cintura, los labios unidos, perderse en el misterio de la vida' (IV, 702). This is pure fairy-tale material. Also worthy of note is the way in which Carmina's description is built around the colour red and the element of fire. This type of characterisation, which in Iluminada's case is based on the colours white and black and the play of light and darkness, is extended to Colás who is identified with the air and the wind. Hence the allusion to Carmina 'bebiéndose los vientos' (IV, 676).

After Juan, Colás is perhaps the most important character in the novel and it is through him that the themes of the work are given their most intellectual treatment. Amorós calls him 'un personaje-conciencia, que sirve al autor como definidor de los demás y de la situación, además de ser portavoz de sus ideas' (2, 367). In the early part of the novel Juan's only real relationship is with Colás, 'un sobrino que criaba consigo' (IV, 544). This adopted son, whom the narrator describes as 'muy despejado y observador' (IV, 564), is the centre of gravity of Juan's whole life. Ayala's portrayal of him shows a co-ordination of physical and mental traits. Slightly dehumanised, 'un mozo espigado, cenceño; brazos largos, de gorila; las coyunturas de los huesos, en rodillas, codos, muñecas, y nudillos,

saledizas, nudosas; desmadejado de miembros; los movimientos, habitualmente tardos, y de pronto vivaces, nerviosos, como sacudidas galvánicas' (IV, 565), he is unconventional in his attitudes. Contemplative and introspective, he has a spontaneous and lively imagination. There are two sides to his personality: 'Era propenso al entusiasmo y asimismo al tedio. Ahora se enardecía, luego se descorazonaba' (IV, 565). Recognising himself to have been born with 'la psicología del insatisfecho' (IV, 567), Colás has something of the nature of the 'perturbado' of the Generation of 1898, except that in the end he finds an equilibrium and a set of satisfactory values. His case is more one of romantic disillusionment than of metaphysical despair. His talent for music and acrobatics, aesthetic and entertaining pursuits, is in keeping with the lightness of his character, his unwillingness to take life too seriously, his vagabond nature: 'Esto es lo que me place, vivir flotando, de aquí acullá . . . Rodar por los caminos. Cada día nuevos semblantes: en el cielo, en la tierra, en los hombres. Extranjero para todos; todos extranjeros para mí' (IV, 566). This is the basic incompatibility between Juan and Colás, 'dos personajes, de opuesto temperamento y textura espiritual distinta' (IV, 569). Juan's sense of duty, responsibility and belief in free will is challenged by Colás's fatalism: '¿Quién es dueño de sí? Vamos adonde el destino nos empuja. Inútil resistir. Soy fatalista' (IV, 580). It is this outlook which inspires Iluminada's description of him as 'el hijo del aire' (IV, 581) with a longing for freedom which Juan wishes to deny him. Where Juan seeks permanent and stable relationships, Colás is happier without bonds. His character offers a further illustration of Ayala's interest in human psychology, especially in the duality of the conscious and unconscious mind. Ayala's thinking here is again part of his total view of reality as consisting of opposing parts. Colás experiences a split between action and desire: 'No soy libre. Nunca lo seré. Quiero una cosa y hago la contraria sin querer. ¿Por qué? ¿Lo entiendo yo mismo? Una fuerza irresistible me ofusca e impele. Cuando acuerdo y quiero retroceder es ya tarde. Todo se ha consumado' (IV, 599). Here he introduces a central theme of the novel: man's life is part of an overall design which he does not understand or perceive. The emotional estrangement of Colás and Juan, Herminia's rejection of Colás and his subsequent departure for the colonies,

are a necessary part of the process that will lead Juan to marry Herminia and discover his repressed nature. The mysterious workings of the mind, and Colás's sudden switches of mood, are given as the reasons why Colás so readily accepts the new situation. He had loved Herminia as an ideal, lacking as he was in real emotional experience. Having resolved his inner life through his new relationship with Carmina, Colás can take a more positive part in the narrative. He again becomes really significant on St John's Night when, in the town of Mañas, he consoles Herminia, Carmen and Lino, and with his unconventional philosophy gets them to see their problems in a new light. Guided by instinct rather than reason— 'Ni ahora ni nunca medito lo que he de hacer. Me dejo llevar de mis impulsos. Lo que ha de ser, será. Soy fatalista' (IV, 743)—he brings Juan and Herminia face to face. His conviction that everything is fated for a preordained end governs his conduct until the end of the novel. He explains his thinking to Juan:

> Todos los sucesos de aquí abajo están encadenados y regidos por una razón misteriosa. Muchas veces me he preguntado a qué razón o finalidad, tanto tiempo impenetrable, obedecía el hecho, sin motivo y arbitrario por las trazas de que usted me hubiera recogido y criado como hijo . . . Todo, todo estaba enderezado a una finalidad, desde el principio, ineluctable. (IV, 746)

Colás, then, provides an intellectual perspective on all that has taken place and his views, taken together with those of Juan, explore the relationship between reason and unreason, free will and predestination, the individual and the universal, intellect and life. The contrast between the two men, and the equal validity of their respective positions, is likened by Iluminada to two different kinds of tree: 'Veo el carácter de usté como una encina. El huracán la hace bramar, pero no la mueve. Se romperá antes que desarraigarse. Colás es una palmera. Se doblará por el viento hasta dar con la frente en el polvo. Pero tampoco se desarraiga. Ni se rompe' (IV, 779). Man responds to life in terms of his own experience and nature and this belief leads naturally to the exercise of tolerance in one's dealings with others. Juan and Colás are radically different on the surface, but we sympathise with them both.

Colás's final contribution is in the *Parergon*, where he formulates

an important distinction between reason and life. He is attracted by the existence of the irrational: 'No puedo resistir el hechizo que sobre mí ejerce todo lo irrazonable y disparatado . . . Me place, me fascina lo absurdo . . .La vida es un absurdo delicioso' (IV, 784). This is something which reason can never comprehend, for it reduces life to demonstrable laws based on past experience. Life, on the other hand, is all future, all potential, and reason holds no sway over it. Moreover all men can share the products of reason, ideas and principles, without these being diminished within the individual. Not so life which is each individual's 'razón de ser'. What is really individual cannot be shared with others, nor can they experience it. Colás here asserts the primacy of what is unique to the individual: 'Mi arquetipo congénito, la idea original, el ideal de mi existencia, mi irracionalidad, mi vida' (IV, 786). Colás, then, while recognising sameness, asserts difference. The great man recognises the infinite diversity of human life, the great artist expresses it:

> El hombre es tanto más inteligente en la medida que acierta a *justificar* fuera de sí, en los demás hombres, el mayor número de vidas individuales, el mayor repertorio de razones de la sinrazón, la cantidad más extensa de irracionalidades, así como el hombre es más artista en la medida que acierta a sentir y hacer sentir, o sea, expresar, con la mayor intensidad su irracionalidad, su vida propia, y otras irracionalidades y vidas ajenas, cuantas más mejor, que viene a ser como multiplicar para los demás hombres las dimensiones y goce de su respectiva vida, la de cada cual. (IV, 786)

It is in the *Parergon* that Colás comes into his own, and his views enjoy equal status with those of Juan. Taken together, they represent Ayala's thinking on life and literature, a statement of his liberalism, his openness to the fullness of life's possibilities.

The last character to be dealt with, Herminia, is likewise inseparable from Juan but whereas Colás exists to present Juan's story from an intellectual view, Herminia acts as a direct parallel in that she, like him, undergoes a process of progressive enlightenment, a steady development towards maturity.

Herminia is not mentioned until the novel is well advanced, and then only as the girl who has rejected Colás. It is this which first brings her into contact with Juan who, convinced as he is of the

perfidy of all women, plans to take revenge. For most of the first part of the novel she remains in the shadows, arousing only Juan's antipathy. This aversion is of course only a mask for more complex and deep-seated emotions which become apparent towards the end of the *Adagio* where her resemblance to Engracia is first noticed: 'el mismo fino óvalo, la misma suave piel de cera, los mismos ojos de aceituna, opacos' (IV, 635-6). From this point onwards, Herminia emerges as a character and a force in the novel. She calmly unravels her feelings for Juan, Colás and Vespasiano, those for Juan, though negative, being the strongest, 'terror y repugnancia' (IV, 643). This is part of Ayala's portrayal of the paradoxical psychology of his two protagonists, which Iluminada perceives. Juan's aversion for women is una confusión de amor ciego y pavura' (IV, 564), an analysis which is similar to that made of Herminia's emotions: 'Herminia dice que siente miedo y repugnancia de Tigre Juan: bonísimo síntoma. Lo que Herminia siente es vértigo hacia Tigre Juan; un poder de atracción que la domina y que no puede contrarrestar si no es encastillándose en una proporcionada voluntad de repulsión' (IV, 653). Herminia has already sensed that Juan is in love with her, as her ensuing conversation with Iluminada reveals, but she prefers to shun reality, to falsify it in order to seek happiness: 'a la verdad que me lastima, prefiero la mentira que me halaga' (IV, 661). Iluminada explicitly relates Herminia's present situation to the traditional fairy-tale of Beauty and the Beast (IV, 662), and there is no doubt that on one level *Tigre Juan* and *El curandero de su honra* follow the pattern of that tale, which is usually interpreted as symbolising woman's overcoming her fear of male sexuality. On their wedding night, man's animality is evident in lines like 'Se oía el resuello, de fiera con calentura, de Tigre Juan' (IV, 689). This fear makes Herminia seek the ambiguous sexuality of Vespasiano and repress her true emotions.

The second part of the novel charts the painful process whereby the characters reach true understanding. In Herminia's case this takes the form of appearing to accept her fate as Juan's wife while knowing all the time that she will eventually escape: 'se rebelaba contra el orden establecido y se proponía a destruirlo' (IV, 674). This rebellion is a necessary step in her enlightenment, for love is experienced first of all as privation. She discovers the perfidy of Vespasiano

and compares it with the true worth of Juan. It only remains for her to discover herself: '¿Me entiendo yo misma, acaso?' she asks Vespasiano (IV, 718). Herminia undergoes an experience akin to a religious conversion. She confesses her guilt and seeks redemption through death: 'Le agradeceré que dé muerte a mi cuerpo, con que mi alma reviva' (IV, 728). When she and Juan are reconciled residual guilt remains. She has a desire to be humiliated by Juan, to be made to suffer, to live in perpetual fear of losing him (IV, 782). However implausible the language of these characters may be, however much they may have metaphorical and symbolic significance, there can be no doubt about the psychological realism with which they are drawn. This is nowhere more apparent than in the treatment of the main character, Tigre Juan.

For this reason it is difficult to accept totally Weber's view that the characters in *Tigre Juan* and *El curandero de su honra* 'are not believable persons living in a real world but actors performing in rigidly prescribed roles' (*13*, 34). One is left rather with an awareness of their curious hybrid nature as persons and archetypes which can be explained, I think, only in terms of the tension between the novel's inherent mimeticism and the author's artistic self-consciousness. Edmund Wilson has argued that 'The real elements, of course, of any work of fiction are the elements of the author's personality . . . his personages are personifications of the author's impulses and emotions, and the relations between them in his stories are the relationships between these.'[9] In other words, the author's vision splits into various attributes which are embodied in characters. An analogy with Ayala's fictional treatment of mental life is illuminating here. In dealing with the workings of the mind, he is not concerned to create the illusion of inner reality but rather gives it material form. He avoids on the whole techniques such as stream-of-consciousness and instead orders the character's thoughts and feelings and objectifies them, turning them into images which explain them by logical association and methodical analysis. In similar fashion, the conflicts in the author's perception of reality are represented in different characters, explored and resolved in

---

[9] *Axel's Castle. A Study in the Imaginative Literature of 1870-1930.* First published in 1931. Quotation from Fontana edition (London, 1974), p. 143.

their interaction. In a Realist novel this kind of relationship is obscured, for the literary work directs attention to external reality and not to the author's consciousness. Ayala keeps his novel ambivalently poised between the two. His characters enjoy a measure of autonomy which permits them to act as models of real people, but when the author calls attention to their essential fictionality by arranging them in patterns of significance based on artistic order and symmetry, their solidity as individuals dissolves and they are united in the single imaginative vision from which they emerged. When this occurs, the presence of the creating mind is shown to be the principal unifying feature of the work.

V The Character and Psychology of Tigre Juan

The opening pages of *Tigre Juan*, as well as, in the words of Walter Starkie, 'unfolding a picture of the tedious vacuity of life in a provincial town',[1] have the effect of reminding the reader how much interest in fiction derives from the basic human need for gossip, the desire to know of the private lives of other people. In Pilares, Tigre Juan's private life is stubbornly resistant to the scrutiny of others and part of the appeal of the novel is that it allows us access to this normally impenetrable world. We are, of course, seeking more than mere facts, for the real value of fiction is that it liberates us from our own restricted vision by imaginatively extending our experience. The novel has traditionally done this by revealing and exploring character, although the twentieth century has been generally less approving of this approach. Whereas many great nineteenth-century novels are named after their most important characters, Galdós's *Fortunata y Jacinta*, Tolstoy's *Anna Karenina*, Flaubert's *Madame Bovary*, the twentieth century has, on the whole, preferred more metaphorical titles, Unamuno's *Niebla*, Henry James's *The Golden Bowl*, Gide's *La Porte étroite*. Criticism has tended to see characters as personifications of the author's own emotions and impulses and therefore subordinate to the overall effect of a novel. This argument has much to commend it and certainly it is not possible to analyse *Tigre Juan* and *El curandero de su honra* without taking into account the way in which the novel functions as a verbal artefact in which character is only one of several constituent parts. But a novel is such a large and complex structure that it is doubtful whether a reader can hold all of it in his mind as an aesthetic whole. He is more likely to retain an impression of a person and discuss a novel in the first place by reference to the characters and their behaviour. While critics have had misgivings about the plausibility of Ayala's methods of characterisation, they have been surprisingly in accord

1 Introduction to his English translation of the novel, *Tiger Juan* (New York, 1933), p. 19.

in recognising the centrality of Tigre Juan to our novel. Maruxa Salgués Cargill and Julián Palley feel that *Tigre Juan* and *El curandero de su honra* 'is probably [Ayala's] most successful novel in terms of the creation of a living and unforgettable protagonist, at war with himself and with his environment' (*10*, 399). Eugenio de Nora concurs that in the novel we encounter 'al más recio e inolvidable de los tipos creados por el autor', arguing that 'hay en él un poderío, una concentración maciza de fuerzas que se impone' (*7*, 506-7). It is Tigre Juan who is most fully drawn, whose life and psychological motivation are most fully established. It is he who changes as the story develops and who most engages our interest and sympathy. In short, he embodies the total vision of the novel. He exists for it, and it for him. Characterisation is the portrayal of man, the events of his life, his condition and circumstances, his relationships, his innermost feelings and thoughts. Ayala neglects none of these, for Juan is located in space, developed in time and analysed in depth. Setting, story and psychology are inseparable.

Julio Matas has called attention to the dramatic nature of Ayala's characterisation: 'Ayala prefiere describir a los personajes, cuando aparecen, mediante un retrato casi completo, como de acotación de pieza dramática, al cual poco se añade después que no esté ya contenido en él' (*6*, 169). Description of characters is rarely straight-forward for it usually functions as part of characterisation. A simple reference to Juan's stall being permanent, while those of the traders around him are dismantled when their business is complete, acts as a pointer to his character: his need for stability. The outward description of Tigre Juan is apparently picturesque, but it is intended to suggest the duality of the man. From the waist up, he dresses 'a lo artesano' and from the waist down 'como un labriego de la región' (IV, 553). There is an incongruity in dress which may be indicative of some inner discord, a marriage of incompatible parts. There is a hint, then, that Juan's nature may be in some way split. Implied too is a marked individuality or even eccentricity which the ensuing description (IV, 553-4) confirms. Ayala endows him with animal-like qualities: 'ojos de gato montés', 'pelambre . . . como montera pastoril de piel de borrego', and dehumanises him, 'fruncía las cejas con metódico ritmo y rapidez . . . este recio capacete piloso resbalaba, de una pieza, hacia delante y hacia atrás, como lubrificado, sobre la gran bola del cráneo . . . el pescuezo flaco, rugoso, curtido, avellanado y retráctil . . . el rostro cuadrado, obtuso . . . su piel parecía de cobre pulimentado'. Alongside these physical details, Ayala emphasises certain qualities such as 'energía', 'altivez', 'cólera', 'bárbara', 'ingenua'. Finally, Juan is compared to the legendary figure of Attila the Hun. So in one paragraph, Ayala has viewed his character as a picturesque, eccentric but not especially abnormal person, as possessing characteristics associated with animals and things, and as a larger-than-life heroic figure. The net effect of this is to create in the reader a feeling of ambivalence, for the apparently conventional introduction of the character together with the *costumbrista* details and setting are somewhat at odds with the undeniable humour latent in the description. This humour, which is not very obtrusive in the work, acts as a counterweight to its tragic potential. Thus a rough Asturian stall-keeper assumes the tragedy of a misogynist with irrepressible paternal instincts. Juan emerges as a complex human being, a shy, gruff and inarticulate man, capable of deep emotion but unable to express it adequately. Nowhere is this more clearly seen than in the ritual scene with the children. The apparent roughness with which he treats them is a manifestation of a deep paternal urge (IV, 558). Later, when he tries to console the dying Carmona, his words have the opposite effect (IV, 597). There is, in other words, a person below the surface who cannot get out. The Juan who is projected to the world is not the whole man. In each of the examples cited, Juan's language does not reveal his true nature but conceals and distorts it. This has important repercussions for characterisation. Juan's story is one of striving firstly for self-knowledge and ultimately for self-realisation and much of what he says in the early part of the novel must be regarded as a manifestation of the mask, or *persona*, that obscures the reality underneath. Apparently conventional modes of narration identify the reader with the false Juan while ambivalence is created by a series of narrative strategies. For one thing, the narrator's factual account of Juan's life and daily routine is followed by a multiple outside view of the character through the eyes of those around him. Juan is considered to be rich and avaricious but generous in seeing to his nephew's education. He is noted for his 'claridad' and 'honradez' and inspires a certain fear 'por su traza hosca y carácter insociable'.

Others say he is really 'un bragazas'. Though not interested in women himself, 'despertaba en no pocas mujeres una especie de curiosidad invencible, mezcla de simpatía y atracción' (IV, 556). The fundamental duality in his character, already hinted at in his initial description, appears confirmed in his unusual name, 'Juan Guerra Madrigal; pareja nada compatible de apellidos que, como perro y gato, sorprende ver juntos y concordes' (IV, 556). On the one hand, a man at war with himself and, on the other, seeking peace and harmony. So, omniscient narration, self-revelation through speech and action, the use of significant name and details, affective description and the opinions of others, are all used as instruments of characterisation in the early part of the novel.

Juan is also defined by his relationships with other people for a character acquires life and plausibility only when he is set in an identifiable human context. The treatment of Juan's closest friend, Vespasiano Cebón, and the treatment of the Don Juan myth go hand in hand, and Juan's psychological growth is most significantly measured in his changing attitude to them. Doña Iluminada is the only living woman Juan respects. Colás, his adopted son, is the object of all his paternal affection and indirectly the origin of all his suffering. Nachín de Nacha, a lifelong friend, represents the temptation to flee into the wilds, natural as opposed to urban life in society. Doña Mariquita and don Sincerato Gamborena complete his circle of acquaintances. References to Engracia, Lieutenant Rebolledo and the appearance of Isabel Semprún provide links with the past. These relationships, then, give added depth to the figure of Juan but on another level they represent aspects of his psychological make-up. The prolonged and rather lofty dialogues between the characters in which they conceptualise their feelings and experiences are, as we have seen, the means whereby the major themes of the work are articulated. The function of these dialogues is to raise the experience of the characters to a higher level than the merely personal so that it takes on mythical or archetypal significance. A very ordinary man becomes a vehicle for heroic feelings and this is made acceptable by the transfiguration or trans-mutation through language of the apparently mundane. The accept-ance of a mythological substratum to experience is necessary if the characters and events of this novel are to attain their full significance.

I wish to argue, then, that it is possible to see Juan as a character, that he does stand as a plausible model of human behaviour in a peculiar set of circumstances, but that at the same time, the supporting structure of the novel, its underlying pattern of motifs and associations, its mythological resonances, add a symbolic dimension to the work which is perfectly compatible with its fundamental realism. The link is provided by the psychological development of the principal character.

In so far as Juan's psychology is explored in the early stages of the novel, it is seen purely in terms of the uneasy calm he has imposed on his life and which is disrupted by the first crucial dialogue with Colás. This aspect of Juan's personality is revealed only gradually, firstly as speculation about his past (IV, 557), his misplaced paternal feelings (IV, 558), his sensitivity on questions of marital honour (IV, 554, 559, 560), doña Iluminada's thoughts on his fear of the opposite sex (IV, 564), and of course Juan's own forthright pronouncements on women. By challenging his views on women, Colás attacks Juan at his most vulnerable point and throws him into a state of mental turmoil. In a sense, one could see the novel as an exercise in psychotherapy by means of which the patient confronts his obsession as a first step to overcoming it. The views of the other characters could be interpreted as projections of his own doubts and anxieties which have been repressed. The key to Juan's character is understanding the nature of his repression. His repressed feelings are not of a specifically sexual kind, though they have sexual associations, and they are not to be thought of as necessarily bad in themselves. The fact is that Juan has expelled from his mind painful memories of his first marriage and has constructed a world-view, governed by a rigid set of principles and ideals which have real value in maintaining stability in his emotional life. The image of reality which Juan nourishes is a false one, a delusion, but it is a way of adapting, of coping with the fact that he has become stuck in a particular phase of emotional development. The novel describes the process by which he overcomes this emotional block.

It must be stressed from the outset that there is no concrete evidence that Ayala wrote *Tigre Juan* and *El curandero de su honra* with the work of any particular psychologist in mind. At the same time, it is impossible to read the novel without being aware of its many psychological insights. An obvious case is the delusion, common to schizophrenics, that everyone knows their innermost thoughts. In the presence of doña Iluminada, Tigre Juan was convinced that 'la viuda leía dentro de él todos sus pensamientos como escritura clara, y que le veía, de bulto y en forma sensible, todos sus sentimientos' (IV, 562). The same phenomenon is described later in terms of the well-known dream: 'A veces tenía en sueños una estrafalaria pesadilla; que, sin saber cómo, había salido de casa en paños menores y en traza tan bochornosa se hallaba a la vista de todos los del mercado. Ahora sentíase como si estuviera peor que en paños menores, in *puribus naturalibus*, en cueros, como un recién nacido' (IV, 583). The Swiss psychologist Carl Gustav Jung, whose psychological theories are generally applicable to the character of Tigre Juan, would interpret this as the unconscious compensating for the conscious. The man who is emotionally isolated invents the idea that everyone knows his innermost thoughts. After all, Juan in the market is described as 'insulado, solo, tan próximo a los demás hombres y, sin embargo, tan distante' (IV, 606). The psychological treatment of the characters in the novel is linked to the literary motifs of truth-falsehood, reality-illusion which form a web through the whole work. An outward sign is really an indication of its opposite. Juan's aversion for women is 'una confusión de amor ciego y pavura' (IV, 564); his bursts of anger 'eran inofensivo disfraz de un alma tierna y tímida' (IV, 600). This suggests a division of the personality into different parts. These can be in conflict one with another or they can function as an integrated whole. For this reason, although some of the novel's psychological insights appear Freudian in inspiration, such as the Oedipal nature of the Juan-Herminia-Colás relationship, the novel, both in detail and in overall vision, is totally explicable in Jungian terms as a quest for integration and wholeness. The psychological integration attained by the protagonist is mirrored in the artistic integration of the novel itself. Jungian psychology is interested above all in the development and growth of the individual personality so that it achieves a balance within itself and establishes a harmonious relationship with the whole of life. Such a view is admirably suited to fictional treatment for it can naturally be construed as a progression towards some objective or goal. The supreme goal is that of self-realisation, in Jung's words, 'a consciousness detached from the world',[2] an attitude of acceptance which is in some way religious. Man discovers his own myth and achieves a reconciliation between the conflicting sides of his own nature. As we shall see, Juan's conflict between emotion and social constraint is resolved by transferring it on to a higher level of experience. The poem of the *Coda* sees reality from this superior perspective and acknowledges the existence of God. This is not necessarily the conventional, Christian God but a spiritual, inner experience which Jung would term the Self. This all-embracing concept can be described in religious terms but it can also be represented in art which offers a synthesis of the inner subjective world of the author and external reality. In art man resolves the contradictions of life. There is therefore a close correlation between Ayala's approach to the life of the mind and his thinking on the art of fiction. Man relates to the external world by means of concepts, abstract thought and symbols which manifest themselves in religion, culture and art. Man's image-making capacity, his inner world of fantasy, is essential to successful adaptation to reality and in this respect there is little essential difference between so-called objective myths, works of fiction and apparently subjective delusions. The unconscious plays an important role here for it is complementary to consciousness which requires its co-operation for the full development of the personality. The unconscious is divided into the 'personal unconscious' which is unique to the individual and contains his forgotten experience, subliminal perceptions and so on, and the 'collective unconscious', which is common to all mankind and is the source of universal myths and symbols. It is here that primordial images referred to as archetypes originate. It is easy to see that all three parts of the mind are taken into account in the characterisation of Tigre Juan. The use of existing myths in the novel is an acceptance of Jung's idea of the collective unconscious. Myths, known to

---

[2] Given the nature and scope of this study, I have not attempted to make specific reference to Jung's writings to support my views. Most of Jung's ideas outlined in this chapter are, I think, well-known and my intention is simply to apply them to the character of Tigre Juan. The curious may consult the Routledge & Kegan Paul edition of Jung's *Collected Works*, especially volumes V-IX.

be similar in widely different cultures and periods of history, express man's basic experiences and try to offer explanations of the world in which he finds himself. Myths and religious ideas are therefore closely linked. In trying to give Juan's experience this archetypal quality, Ayala has had to create a figure who is larger than life. This has been recognised by several critics. Francisco Agustín wrote, 'reconoceremos en él al personaje de un bello mito novelesco' (*1*, 214) and 'Andrenio' (Eduardo Gómez de Baquero) commented in an early review of the novel: 'Personaje mítico llamo a Tigre Juan, no porque sea fabuloso, sino porque estando henchido de humanidad, excede de la talla vulgar humana.'[3] The use of myth and archetype, the quest for wholeness, the reconciliation of opposites, and concepts such as individuation, the self-regulating psyche, and the Self, make *Tigre Juan* and *El curandero de su honra* highly susceptible to Jungian analysis.

Juan's problem is his relationship with the opposite sex, and his attitude to women is characterised by the very dualism we find in Jung, the opposing images of woman as destroyer and woman as protector. In mythical terms these are represented respectively as Eve and the Virgin Mary, both of whom are mentioned in the novel. In terms of the character's own experience, the images are projected onto Iluminada on the one hand, and on the negative side onto a complex cluster including for a time both Engracia and Herminia. Frequently, these images take the forms of the fairy godmother and the evil witch. In the novel Iluminada is referred to as the 'hada madrina' (IV, 654), and in a moment of rage Juan calls la Güeya 'bruja' and 'barragana de Satanás' (IV, 603). Juan, culturally conditioned and guilty for his crime, represses the good image and develops the bad. The crisis comes when this particular structure is upset. Jung conceived of the psyche as a play of opposites with psychic energy running, as it were, between two poles. These have a regulating function for when one extreme is reached the energy passes over to its opposite, a phenomenon known as enantiodromia in which, for example, anger suddenly gives way to calm, hatred to affection, and so on. This is what Jung designates the 'self-regulating psyche', a concept which in psychological terms corresponds to the accepted physiological fact that the body is

[3] *El Sol* (Madrid), 13 March 1926.

regulated by an elaborate system of checks by which a tendency to go too far in one direction, in the production of a hormone, for example, is automatically compensated and a proper balance maintained. In this respect, it is significant that Juan can be seen as curing himself, as suggested, albeit humorously, by the title *El curandero de su honra* and his practice of homeopathy (IV, 555). If this is true, Juan's sudden transformation is psychologically valid and not in the least surprising. It undermines the objections of critics like Norma Urrutia, who writes: 'No nos convence, pues, ese Tigre Juan, que odia a la mujer durante ciento ochenta páginas y, bruscamente, como por arte de magia, sucumbe al amor de Herminia' (*12*, 101). Ayala stressed how unreal the misogynist phase actually is, a device designed to disguise the truth. Juan's outspoken condemnation of women is a need to justify and protect himself and the manner in which everything is reshaped and made to conform to his own interpretation of the world is an elaborate delusional system. It is one of the many paradoxes of the novel and in keeping with Ayala's ceaseless probing of polarities in his work. Belarmino and Apolonio are the complementary halves of the same person, the introvert is balanced by the extravert. Jung himself refers to cases of alternation between introversion and extraversion and even cases where lifelong introverts have become extraverts in middle age. In Juan's case the 'good' image of woman had never been completely submerged (IV, 561), and it is in the unconscious that latent possibilities of new life are to be found. What is not present in the conscious attitude is lurking in the unconscious and is sometimes manifested in dreams and fantasies. This aspect of unconscious life is given little attention by Ayala and it is true to say that in the novel unconscious feelings are rendered with more precision than may be thought desirable. However, we join the drama at a point where unconscious emotions are beginning to surface and are therefore experienced in a way that is not strictly speaking unconscious at all; they are rather a surge of wild and chaotic feelings and thoughts which burst into consciousness, 'ansiedades y zozobras, largo tiempo sumisas, amordazadas, y ahora rebeldes de pronto' (IV, 581). So painful are these memories that when they well up Juan tries to rebury them:

Aquella noche, rebulléndose desazonado, hubo de ser sincero consigo mismo . . . Apenas, en un momento de abandono de la voluntad y pérdida de dominio de sí, hizo esta confesión íntima, cuando saltó del camastro, cayó de rodillas y dándose de puñadas en los ojos, murmuraba roncamente. Creyó ver primero una gran mancha roja, y luego un negror poblado de estrellitas rutilantes: 'Aún bramas por la mujer, insensato, como ciervo sediento por el manantial . . . Señor de justicia, Señor de misericordia, ciégame.' (IV, 582)

This craving for blindness is the clearest symptom of Juan's repression. It might be more appropriate to use the term 'dissociation' rather than 'repression' as this would include both conscious and unconscious mental contents. Thoughts and feelings which are considered alien to the personality are rejected or denied. In this respect, it is interesting that men condemn in others what they cannot accept in themselves. Thus Juan is vehemently opposed to Colás's idealisation of women, his desire for freedom from restraint, his assertion of the primacy of instinct. Juan's fears are represented in an image dominated by the colour red which has connotations of passion and violence, and is connected to the motif of blood which recurs in the novel. Together they contain suggestions of death and sacrifice and this is reinforced by the parallel established between Juan and the Christ figure. This mythical parallel of the death and subsequent resurrection of the hero indicates a turning-point in life, the transition from one state to another. The arguments with Colás, the suggestion that he should remarry, the conversations with doña Iluminada bring Juan to a point where he recognises that important aspects of his personality have been neglected and the life he created may well prove unsatisfactory. The trauma of the departure of Colás signals the collapse of his former life: 'Acabóse ayer. Soy un cadáver que anda' (IV, 604). He is born to a second life which is a re-enactment of the first, as several lines make clear: 'Parece como si escomezase a vivir, o séase desandar y recorrer de nuevo el mismo camino' (IV, 611). The vital link with the past is provided by the letter from the wife of his former captain in the Philippines which unlocks the secrets of the past: 'Todo había concluido para él. Sólo cuando algo está definitivamente concluso, su pasado revive y se hace actual, perenne e incorregible. Su propio pasado, que

Tigre Juan suponía abolido, se restauraba íntegro, cuajado en una eternidad de infierno' (IV, 623). Juan becomes Juanín as the story of Engracia and the origins of Juan's obsession are recounted in a flashback. The structuring of the narrative in this way enables the reader to undergo a process of enlightenment similar to that of the character. Viewed thus the novel is essentially dramatic in that both reader and character are brought to the point of recognition. By acting out his own drama the character comes to a proper understanding of the real nature of his role. Re-enactment has a psychological value as the character, hallucinated or hypnotised, envisages his past as a grotesque dance of death in which characters parade before his eyes, taking on their true significance which he had consciously repressed: 'Era para él como el derrumbamiento y catástrofe de un mundo falso, perecedero, mundo de apariencias vanas, por él mismo fabricado, en el cual vivía dormido, trasvolado en un duermevela, tomando por realidades tangibles, los sueños de inmaterial urdimbre' (IV, 629). The recognition that he had created a false view of reality to make it conform to his own inner needs begins the slow and painful process of individuation which is completed only at the end of the novel. The recognition itself has been achieved by the end of the *Adagio* of *Tigre Juan*, that part of the novel that had revealed the basic split in Juan's character. A highly emotional man, Juan is deeply mistrustful of manifestations of sentiment, 'que no gusto de zalamerías, arrumacos y garatusas' (IV, 590). His whole life is a struggle for control: 'me arrebata tal vez una fuerza irresistible que destruye lo que más amo' (IV, 599). What we are discussing here is the importance of unconscious desires and emotions and the difficulty experienced in bringing these into the domain of consciousness. Rather than come to terms with his feelings, especially about women, Juan chose to repress them, with the result that his relationships with others have tended to be frictional or conflictive. Juan's natural instinct is to withdraw into himself: 'Déjenme solo, como apetezco' (IV, 610). Buried in his personal unconscious his emotions gain in strength and intensity and, in a situation of stress, they sweep away reason. Juan's 'murder' of Engracia is a case in point. Placed where it is in the novel this incident, though a flashback, seems a logical consequence of Juan's attitudes and behaviour in the *Adagio*. Because of an inner contradiction, Juan's motives and even the very nature of his actions are unknown to him. As he rushes impulsively towards Colás, the narrator observes: '¿Iba a abrazarle o estrangularle? ¿Qué sabía el? Lo mismo podía resultar lo uno como lo otro' (IV, 603), or earlier 'La onda colérica que le henchía había llegado a un punto de plenitud e inestabilidad, indecisa entre reventar en violencia o replegarse en humedad de ojos' (IV, 600). This instability, intensified by the cataclysmic vision with which the *Adagio* ends, so radically alters Juan's psychological make-up that Ayala suggests that he is another person, though unaware of it. Juan had always been aware of dark and powerful forces deep within himself: 'Aunque oprimido y a medias domesticado, tigre soy y seré hasta que muera' (IV, 571). Jung calls this the 'shadow' which is his archetype for all that primitive, uncontrolled, animal part of man which, in a moment of crisis, can overwhelm the rest of personality. In the first half of the novel, Juan had repressed this aspect of his personality because he felt threatened by it; in the second part he is able to come to terms with it. Thus the second part provides an alternative solution to the problem of adultery which becomes possible because Juan's conscious and unconscious have established a different relationship one with the other. It is not achieved without considerable struggle and suffering.

The recognition of Engracia's innocence, the subsuming of his first wife into the person of Herminia, and his psychological transformation create a transitory state of consciousness in which Juan continues to act in accord with a false, self-engendered, though now altered, vision of the world: 'En el estado de semialucinación en que Tigre Juan se hallaba, no le era hacedero acomodar los sentidos a la realidad de fuera; antes, por el contrario, deformaba y transformaba los datos del mundo externo a fin de incorporarlos al espejismo de su visión interior' (IV, 637). At the centre of this is love for a woman. Men fall in love with what seems to be lacking in themselves. The image of the beloved is therefore initially the expression of a subjective need.

Jung's psychology is decidedly woman-centred. In his writings he refers to the *anima*, man's image of woman, as one of the central archetypes of the mind. This archetype seems to come from three sources: the collective, primordial image of woman which man inherits, man's own experience of woman, and the feminine qualities in himself. The *anima* is frequently associated with water or the earth, she appears to have great power, and is endowed with spiritual value. Woman, by fascinating man erotically, teaches him about emotion and its value and provides a link between the conscious and unconscious mimds. The power of the *anima* may explain the transference of Engracia to Herminia in Juan's mind: he projects his *anima* onto her. Etymologically, *anima* means 'soul' and Jung has described the *anima* as the very soul of man, the essence of his personality. A curiously similar observation is made by Ayala at the beginning of the *Presto*: 'Tigre Juan . . . quedó suplantado en su ser interior e inconsciente por otro ser ajeno: el de Herminia. Ya de allí en adelante no fue él en sí mismo, sino Herminia fue del todo en él' (IV, 637). The *Presto*, then, traces in fine psychological detail Juan's growing love for Herminia. For example, Juan's emotions with regard to Herminia and Colás become entangled. His love for Colás is first transformed into a vengeful hatred towards Herminia, but what Juan thinks is hate is in reality love for her, or at least for the resurrected image of Engracia he has projected onto her. A complex of emotions is gradually and unconsciously re-arranged to allow Juan to maintain a proper psychological balance, as Ayala carefully explains: 'Para él, creer que continuaba odiando a Herminia equivalía, por una inversión sofística del sentimiento, a gozarse en la certidumbre de que Herminia había rechazado a distancia a otro pretendiente, y como éste era Colás, casi su hijo, necesitaba mantener aquel falso odio por no dejar de deleitarse en la certidumbre de su fundamento' (IV, 638). This love-hate equivalence parallels in a striking manner Herminia's subsequent experience: 'El odio a Tigre Juan, ¿no sería mentido, más bien de pasión de amor, miedosa de sí misma, que se resiste a manifestarse?' (IV, 665). In Juan's case certain symptoms do manifest themselves: he tries to dissuade Colás from thinking any more about Herminia, he becomes more generous, his appearance is subtly modified, he treats Carmina with exaggerated courtesy. Under the influence of his unconsious love, Juan enters a new phase of 'optimismo cósmico' in which 'Todas las cosas le seducían; era llevado hacia ellas por un modo de amor nacido de la comprensión. Todo era hermoso. Todo era útil. Todo era bueno' (IV, 647). Juan's love unlocks a whole world not previously apprehended as he finds his place in the total order of things. The earth takes on womanly forms; Carmina becomes a symbol of womanhood. When man represses his feminine side, the *anima* is largely negative. When Juan begins to appreciate woman once again, the feminine side of his nature is developed. Thus he wishes to participate in child-birth, remembering the old Asturian custom of the *covada*, and he takes an active part in caring for his child to the extent of attempting to simulate breast-feeding. This acknowledgement of the feminine side of man, and by implication of the masculine side of woman, is of course the basis of Ayala's interpretation of the Don Juan myth. Don Juan is an arche-typal image in this sense. For Juan he is a saviour or redeemer and is specifically described as such. When a man feels threatened he instinctively seeks someone to blame and at the same time someone to protect or avenge him. This primordial tendency finds expression in Juan's case in his attitudes to women and to Vespasiano. Vespasiano represents something deficient in himself, 'su otra mitad ideal; el otro yo, que él hubiera preferido ser' (IV, 677). Juan's relationships with Vespasiano and with Colás are reverse images of one another and are both immature. In a way, he is emotionally identified with Vespasiano in that he aspires to be like him. He negates his own personality and is absorbed into Vespasiano. On the other hand, he attempts to incorporate Colás, to so dominate him that he destroys his individuality. The novel shows how Juan's process of self-realisation involves the attainment of more mature relationships in which one neither absorbs nor is absorbed by the other. In the *Presto*, then, a subtle readjustment of conscious and unconscious elements takes place. Juan's apparent 'sistema de venganza' is really an elaborate courtship, as the narrator makes clear and doña Iluminada explains in her analysis of the nature of human love. Juan is directed to Herminia via Colás and a bizarre triangle is created. Were Herminia to marry Colás, Juan's love might be sublimated and expressed as paternal affection, but if this did not take place tragedy would be inevitable. Herminia's rejection of Colás, which she ascribes to her fear of Juan, is an instinctive acceptance of this fact. Herminia appears to be repelled by Tigre Juan but this is a defence against being attracted to him: 'Lo que Herminia siente es vértigo hacia Tigre Juan; un poder de atracción que la domina y que no puede contrarrestar si no es encastillándose en una proporcionada voluntad de repulsión' (IV, 653). This repulsion-attraction contradiction must be resolved. Herminia has an instinctive fear of sex which is symbolised in the fairy-tale of Beauty and the Beast. Her *animus*, woman's image of man, is projected onto Vespasiano who is, significantly, mysterious, alluring and mostly absent. Since he is shadowy and distant, it is easy for Herminia to project an image onto him. When she finally confronts him, he loses his power over her and she is able to live with her husband free from her fantasy and infatuation. In a more general sense, Ayala accepts the existence of the *animus* in his observation that women are attracted by what appears strange, remote or inaccessible: 'es propio de la naturaleza femenina inclinarse hacia lo fuero de lo común y perecerse por lo temible y misterioso' (IV, 556). Herminia is fascinated by Juan's enactment of the role of the Calderonian husband, and the news of his dark past is a further incentive to marry him. By the end of the *Presto*, Herminia is able to disentangle her emotions and to categorise the attributes of her various suitors into various aspects of masculine love. Colás, the 'chiquillo', would satisfy her need to dominate; Juan, the 'hombre', her need to be dominated. Vespasiano, meanwhile, offers an escape towards the unknown and his ambiguous sexuality holds out the prospect of seduction without terror. Ironically, the *Presto* ends with Juan eagerly awaiting Vespasiano's return. Gamborena's words recall the theme of the paradoxical nature of reality and seem to underline the irony. But, as events prove, the words have a more profound meaning than at first appears, for Vespasiano's role is eventually interpreted positively as being a necessary stage in the growth of love between the two spouses. The first part of the novel, then, is a study of repression, but by the time the full story is known that repression is seen to have a temporary value. Juan's delusional system, in which every woman is made to conform to his view, is part self-justification, part self-defence, and is interpreted positively as adaptive. In the *Presto*, Juan is moving from one state of consciousness into another. There has been a fundamental change, but the mind copes with it only slowly through subterfuge and symbol.

El curandero de su honra begins with Juan's recognition of his love and the fixing of the date for the marriage. The initiative, paradoxically, is passed to Herminia, whose outer calm is only a mask. The archetypal woman, clearly implied in the references to Eve, Eden, and seduction by the serpent, frustrates man's plans. In this way the novel is made to transcend the particularities of time and place and function as an account of universal experience expressed in Christian and pagan mythology. The myth of Adam and Eve was one of the principal sources for Juan's belief in the perfidy of woman and her role in mankind's fall. Now that his opinion is changing, now that he is overcoming his obsession, Herminia is about to act in complete conformity with the Eve archetype. Vespasiano insinuates himself into Juan's potential paradise in which the past is obliterated. Locked in his own world, Juan is oblivious of the danger and, unable to express his love for Herminia, entrusts Vespasiano with the task. He faces a double betrayal by wife and friend. The security which appears to surround his new life is seen when he claims that Isabel Semprún means nothing to him: 'Su nueva vida era tan densa que al pronto le tapaba el pasado. Su presente era un paraíso con altísimo cerco, cuya entrada defendía una esfinge' (IV, 686). The complexities of his emotions are most clearly seen with regard to the return of Colás. Once the initial readjustment of relationships is made and the characters recognise the Oedipal implications of their love and overcome them (IV, 693-8), matters appear reasonably simple. Colás gives Juan an outlet for his emotion which is inhibited in the presence of Herminia. Colás's departure had been instrumental in leading Juan to Herminia; now his return breaks Juan's spiritual isolation. For Herminia, Colás's return is a welcome distraction in her married life, but it is also a possible link between her and Tigre Juan. At the same time, Juan notes Herminia's natural gravitation towards Colás and secretly hopes he will leave. He will not of course admit this to himself and even transfers his desire to Colás and reprimands him for thinking of leaving (IV, 700). This kind of psychological insight reveals the contrary impulses to which human beings are frequently subject. A simple example is when Juan is both fascinated and frightened by his conversation with doña Iluminada: 'Le corría por el cuerpo un hormiguillo o anhelo acucioso de marcharse, pero no acertaba a poner punto final a la charla' (IV, 591). When Colás and Carmina elope, Juan is 'henchido de un sentimiento promiscuo, entre la satisfacción y la contrariedad' (IV, 702), a characteristically dual response. For Herminia, on the other hand, Colás's flight arouses her own latent desire to escape, a desire which becomes a veritable obsession. The pattern traced by the novel, then, is one of alternate bouts of tension and relaxation, of revolt and resignation, crisis and contentment. We see underlying this an archetypal pattern of departure followed by return, initiated now by Colás and imitated by Herminia, which represents a phase in life's spiritual journey.

As if intuitively aware of Herminia's absence, Juan, in the *Adagio*, reflects on the related ideas of death, loss and free will, and works his way through the varying interpretations of honour. He begins to shift the centre of gravity of the male-female relationship from the man to the woman. He appears as a soul in conflict, seeking both blindness and enlightenment, unable to find peace within himself. This psychological instability reveals the need for a more intense or severe therapeutic shock to reintegrate his personality completely. His anxiety and excitement reach a feverish pitch on hearing of Herminia's pregnancy, and Nachín de Nacha warns him of the danger of ending up 'en el malicomio o el presidio' (IV, 723). The shock of Herminia's departure initiates a phase of regression. He returns to a state prior to that of loving Herminia: 'Vuelto estoy en mi antiguo ser, que yo mismo me asusto y apenas me reconozco' (IV, 730-1).   Psychological theories are curiously set alongside traditional ideas and pagan superstitions. For example, the close connection between the physical and the mental is seen in the idea of blood-letting which acts as an emotional purgation, and in Nachín de Nacha's reference to the humours, which can be vomited out (IV, 731).

Juan's final emotional release comes, of course, on St John's Night when the whole theme of blindness-enlightenment is given its fullest expression. The feast of St John (24 June) has special significance for Tigre Juan as it is his saint's day (San Juan Bautista), but in addition to this the night before the feast is traditionally associated with lovers. In Asturias particularly, rituals, essentially pagan in origin and related to love and fertility, are performed. Fire and water are prominent elements signifying male and female respectively. The young men jump through the flames of the bonfires courting death and then re-emerge transformed, while the young girls seek out the cool natural water to which they offer a red rose. Then at the end of the ritual male and female unite as all the elements interpenetrate in an image of harmony and completeness: 'los contrarios elementos, tierra y aire, fuego y agua, se penetraban y trasfundían en amoroso consorcio: la tierra se evaporaba y el aire se adensaba: el fuego se atemperaba y el agua hervía' (IV, 753). These natural forces signify the depth of passion existing in Juan and Herminia and their fusion prefigures their eventual reconciliation as parts of the whole of creation. One feature of characterisation in the novel is the association of certain characters with a specific natural element. Thus Colás is in various ways related to the wind and the air: 'hijo del aire ... el viento reclamaría sus derechos de paternidad' (IV, 581). Juan himself is associated with fire: 'el fuego que me consume' (IV, 730), 'Soy un volcán' (IV, 731), 'devorándose a sí propio como una pira' (IV, 732). The Midsummer ritual with its sexual symbolism represents an irrational union of opposites and therefore offers an image of wholeness. In *Las máscaras*, Ayala recalls the myth, discussed in Plato's *Symposium,* that there were originally three sexes, male, female and hermaphrodite. When Zeus decreed that each should be split in half, the sexes were left incomplete and each felt the desire to seek out the other half. Sexual union therefore becomes an image of completeness (III, 367-8). Juan's moment of illumination comes at midnight when, hallucinated, he speaks to images of Engracia and Herminia while reality appears as a 'sueño evanescente' and the world 'se disintegraba y fluía, fluía con fugitivas mudanzas'. The process of destruction and creation which the whole universe seems to undergo is an image or correlative of Juan's psychological disintegration and then re-integration: 'Contemplé el cielo por una rendija y volvime del revés. El rayo de la revelación hendió mi carne' (IV, 739). Juan arrives at this state not by any rational means. Illumination seems to have come from a source beyond consciousness. Juan is purged of the past as Nachín, in a further Midsummer ritual, baptises him in the early-morning dew, long thought to have curing powers. Pagan and Christian symbolism combine to link an individual moment of psychological insight to primitive forms of cultural expression.

We can see, therefore, that Juan's whole experience has a religious dimension in the sense that its inspiration seems to come from a source outside himself or at least outside consciousness. In Jung's account of the individuation process the attainment of a new level of psychological insight brings with it a feeling of unity with the whole of life, an acknowledgement of the existence of something beyond or greater than the individual. There is, in fact, a background of religious imagery and allusion to the novel which is clearly apparent in the close connection established between love, suffering and sacrifice. When Colás leaves for the first time, Juan interprets this as the collapse of his whole life: 'Acabóse ayer. Soy un cadáver que anda' (IV, 604). A religious parallel is evident here, death followed by resurrection. Juan climbs the neighbouring hills 'como si aspirase llegar por último a la cima de su calvario y epílogo de su redención' (IV, 605). In the mountain hermitage, he acts out his own 'Agony in the Garden' using the words from the Gospel: 'Señor, señor, ¿por qué me abandonaste?' (IV, 606). When Juan first recognises his guilt, religious vocabulary is again employed: '¡Condenado estoy! . . . ¿Habrá salvación para mí? . . . infierno . . . purgatorio . . . Colás me redimió . . . expiación . . . arrepentimiento . . . confesión . . . absuelvas' (IV, 630-1). Carmina's kiss on Juan's cheek is like 'un divino estigma visible' (IV, 612). Nachín de Nacha, on a more superstitious level, tries to convince Juan of the existence of another world, a 'país encantao', peopled with 'animes e creatures del otro mundo, xanas, trasgo, duende, huestia' (IV, 610). Images and figures are created by man to represent common human experiences. Herminia's life, although treated in much less detail, also undergoes significant change and the Cross acts as a symbol of this. On her wedding-night 'Herminia estaba caída sin sentido en el lecho, cara al cielo, abiertos los brazos como crucificados al tálamo.' The next sentence seems to confirm that the archetypal pattern of death and rebirth is present here: 'Moría la luz artificial del quinqué y nacía la aurora' (IV, 691). In an early morning scene soon afterwards, Juan's kisses fix her 'a los leños del tálamo igual que en una cruz' (IV, 707). Birth and death are of course brought together, as I have indicated, in the St John's Night ritual. It is the image of blood which fuses the idea of death and sacrifice with love and fulfilment. When Juan hears of Herminia's pregnancy, he accidentally cuts himself and thinks of their blood being mingled in that of the child. Juan's occupation as a 'curandero' leads him, in a parodying echo of Calderón's play, to bleed himself, first as an attempt at suicide and then more positively as a purgation of his own bad blood: 'necesitaba sangrar y descongestionar su alma' (IV, 754). As doña Iluminada makes clear, Juan undergoes a symbolic death and re-birth: 'Don Juan, el tigre, ha muerto. Bien muerto está. Ha renacido otro Don Juan' (IV, 756). Juan's search for meaning in life required the co-operation of both the conscious and unconscious parts of the mind so that after a prolonged period of suffering and struggle, of progression and regression, he reaches an inner understanding, a sense of wholeness, the realisation of the archetype of the Self which is akin to the experience of God. Thus, as well as harmonising all the contradictions of his nature, he experiences an intimate relationship with the whole of life: 'Su conciencia se amplifica, se infiltra y diluye en las cosas, se confunde, con un escalofrío sagrado, en la conciencia cósmica' (IV, 769). The unity and continuity of life is seen in the fact that as one life, don Sincerato, is departing the world, a new life, Mini, is being born. Indeed, the union of the individual with the totality is present also in the song of la Güeya to Mini: 'dirigiéndose desesperados requiebros de amor—amor a la vida—que parecían dilatarse en un eco extinguible, desde la noche de los siglos. La vieja rugosa y el tiernísimo infante formaban un grupo comparable al pámpano y el sarmiento, o bien la vida naciente en el regazo de la tradición' (IV, 761). The profoundly religious nature of this concept is the subject of the poem with which the *Coda* ends. Human and divine love are equated and paternity is compared with divine creation. All elements of human life are purposeful. For Juan to reach this state of awareness and acceptance, a long and mysterious process had to be undergone. The culminating experience, characterised by a sense of purpose and fulfilment, is not capable of being explained in rational terms, but manifests itself in paradox. In the poem we read that 'Lo torpe guía hasta lo honesto./El dolor desemboca en la alegría./La fealdad empuja hacia lo bello' (IV, 770). The exploration of paradoxes and contradictions is continued into the *Parergon*. Colás, considering that man is rational and irrational at the same time, argues that reason is common to all men whereas what is unique to the individual is his 'razón de ser; y esta razón de ser es en cada caso la razón de la sinrazón' (IV, 785). There seems to be a convergence here between the ideas of Juan and Colás. Colás aspires to the discovery of his 'arquetipo congénito, la idea original, el ideal de mi existencia, mi irracionalidad, mi vida' (IV, 786). His life is a quest for origins, Juan's is a pursuit of ends: 'En la distancia que cada criatura se aproxima más o menos a la perfección, encierra al respective, más o menos razón de ser. ¿Cuál es la razón de ser del hombre? Hacerse lo más hombre posible' (IV, 789). This dynamic conception of personality is what emerges most strongly from the story of Tigre Juan, and when Juan's and Colás's ideas are put together, man is seen as both archetype and potential, created out of some common mould but capable of developing his own unique characteristics.

We can see, then, that the characterisation of Tigre Juan is twofold. He is presented initially as a recognisable human being, living in a specific environment and having a framework of human relationships. On one level, his story is that of a man obsessed with fidelity in marriage who overcomes his obsession through the trans-forming power of love. In the course of the novel, he acquires archetypal significance as his experience is raised to a higher plane than the normal. Mundane reality is transformed by the power of art into something transcendent, for Ayala treats his theme on a realistic and social level and then refracts it through literature and myth. It is the psychological portrayal of the principal protagonist which fuses the two levels of reality and myth. The split in his personality is healed by symbolic means as he draws on the resources of his unconscious mind which is partly expressed through arche-typal images and collective rituals. The final aim of the individual is the realisation of his total personality which involves recognising and coming to terms with characteristics in himself that had been consistently rejected. Juan's attempt to be other than he was led to internal conflict, inner disharmony and emotional isolation. On St John's Night he recognises this: 'Yo permanezco a solas, como una roca, sin alteración y sin existencia' (IV, 734). In other words, isolation inevitably leads to the disintegration and death of the personality, for paradoxically one is most truly oneself when one accepts the need for a relationship with others. The awareness that one is valued and accepted by others is a prerequisite for self-esteem and self-acceptance. The story of Tigre Juan's search for love involves a rejection of any idea of man's self-sufficiency. It is an assertion that man needs others if he is to be fully at peace with himself.

VI Pérez de Ayala and the Practice of Fiction

It has been a persistent theme of this study that *Tigre Juan* and *El curandero de su honra* attempts to combine two qualities, fidelity to experience and artistic self-consciousness, which many readers would regard as incompatible. The musical orchestration of the novel's parts, the structuring of the narrative on the basis of images or even single words, the imitation of myth, the arrangement of literary motifs, the use of poetry, play format, and parallel columns, all naturally point to an aesthetic order which sets form over life, pattern over contingency, art over reality. Ayala seemed to recognise the introspective nature of his mature novels when he described them as 'universos cerrados sobre sí mismos'.[1] Criticism has tended to accept the novels on these terms and argue that artistic treatment is more important than any attempt at realism. But no reading of *Tigre Juan* and *El curandero de su honra* can fail to reveal the extent to which this artistic order is compromised by the inclusion and indeed assertion of all that stands against it, reality, life, contingency. Although he does not articulate his misgivings in this way, the experience of such an inner contradiction may have led Julio Matas to say that the work gives the impression of an 'obra maestra manquée' (*6*, 155).

The answer to this dilemma must lie in ascribing to art the function of integrating experience, of bringing man's inner world of imagination into a more harmonious relationship with external reality. Few readers would accept that the classification of 'love-story' is an adequate description of *Tigre Juan* and *El curandero de su honra*. This is not simply because the term evokes connotations of eroticism on the one hand and sentimentality on the other. In fact, the sexual aspect of the love of Juan and Herminia is only obliquely referred to in the novel. The theme of love is explored in psychological terms as a quest for integrity within the individual personality through the development of a mature relationship with

[1] Interview with Luis Calvo in *ABC* (Madrid), 23 November 1930.

another person. When this state has been attained, the individual experiences a sense of fulfilment and inner harmony which is commonly accepted as a characteristic of aesthetic experience. The novel is a poetic myth which finds in the experience of love and the practice of art the very meaning of life itself. It is the attempt to achieve the experience of wholeness through the appreciation of form which encourages Ayala to depart from the techniques of Realism and Naturalism: ' "Novela realista" y más "novela naturalista" es contradicción en los términos o pleonasmo fútil. Si realidad en bruto o tal como es, ya no es una novela, y si es novela tiene que ser realidad, pero realidad esencial; una proyección o extracto superrealista, y sobre-naturalista, en cierto modo.'[2] Ayala seems to feel that nineteenth-century Realism is precariously close to the point where the gap between art and reality will be bridged and art as such cease to exist. This view raises the related questions of the nature of fictional experience and the potentialities and function of literary language. When we read a novel, we surrender to a particular use of language which is intended to convey a particular view of experience. Novels are linguistic systems intended to persuade and there is a paradox here at the very heart of the novel which is most acutely felt in Realist fiction. The presentation of reality implies objectivity yet the author must see his material in a personal, subjective way and his selection, ordering and communication of that material will persuade the reader to see it in the same way. To disguise this fact, the Realists strive for the illusion of reality by adopting a technique of impersonality. It is precisely in the artful resolution of the subjective-objective contradiction that we encounter the major discoveries and achievements of Realist aesthetics. Ayala, in the observation quoted above, clearly simplifies the relationship between Realist fiction and reality, but he is correct in calling attention to the artistic problems posed by subjectivity. His solution, if it can be called a solution, is to acknowledge the subjective element in creation to the highest degree by adopting a self-conscious mode of presentation.

It is usually argued that by exposing the contrivance behind the work, by calling attention to the artist's own creative activity, self-conscious narration blurs the limits of fiction and reality and

[2] *Principios y finales de la novela*, p. 41.

shows the ground between them to be shifting. Deliberate displays of fictionality show up the insubstantiality of the real world and exploit the difference between what things really are and what we think they are. Fiction and reality are shown to be interchangeable in a world where everything is relative, nothing permanent or fixed. Novels which proceed in this way create ontological insecurity in the reader by throwing him into a strange world in which the categories with which he thought he was familiar, such as time and space, are deliberately inverted. By such devices the reader's own world is undermined. The fact that Ayala believed that truth has many facets and that each individual sees only a small part of it, a theme which he explored in *Belarmino y Apolonio*, tends to identify him with those writers who maintain that no reality exists outside individual consciousness. Ayala's novels, however, are radically different from those of many of his contemporaries. We do not, for example, find in them the anguished intellectuals, the alienated beings who people the world of so much modern fiction. Rather we encounter humble characters who eventually find fulfilment in their personal lives. On the simple level of plot, Ayala's novels are unmistakably optimistic. But in a wider sense, Ayala seems to believe that fiction should serve not to loosen man's grip on reality but to tighten it. The art of fiction provides a means of linking consciousness and external reality: 'El arte del novelista consiste en la proporción inexcusable, en sus rasgos sustantivos, con que andan enlazados la realidad externa y el mundo interior; lo que es y como lo siente y piensa cada cual; la visión de los ojos y lo subjetivo; psicología viva de diversos seres.'[3] Fiction is not reality; it is a representation of reality in words, and the art of the novelist is an art of stylisation: 'claro está que una novela está elaborada con la misma materia de que está hecha la vida; mas la suya es realidad quintaesenciada, por ser vida revivida, y no se puede revivir la vida en su extensión, sino en su intensidad'.[4] If a novel is made of the same substance as life, we shall respond to it in terms of characters, actions and so on, and the novelist's language will encourage us to do so. Intensity, however, is a quality

[3]   *Principios y finales de la novela*, p. 25.

[4]   *Principios y finales de la novela*, p. 44.

we associate with a poetic use of language which sharpens our awareness and heightens our sensitivity. In following one man's drama of
consciousness, the novel functions on a level higher than the normal
and attains heights of poetic intensity when the character experiences
piercing moments of illumination which appear to put him in contact with the whole of creation. This submerging of the individual
within the greater whole without the sacrifice of his uniqueness,
without his transformation into pure symbol, is a major artistic
achievement of *Tigre Juan* and *El curandero de su honra*. Behind it
lies a vision that can only be described as religious.

The existence of a reality beyond the individual had been acknowledged from the beginning of the novel. Colás is the main proponent
of the fatalist attitude: 'Lo que ha de ser, será' (IV, 743); Herminia
fled 'porque estaba de Dios' (IV, 742). Juan, who had consistently
asserted free will and the individual's responsibility for his own
actions, is credited with the idea expressed in the poem of the *Coda*:
'No sospechas que tienes la ruta trazada./Y Dios ha sido el ingeniero'
(IV, 769), which echoes Colás's reference to 'La voluntad descono-
cida que gobierna los destinos humanos' (IV, 746). This is, of course,
no grim determinism, for the feeling that all elements of existence
are purposeful is a source not of anguish but of consolation. Freedom consists not in directing the course of one's life but in adapting
to it. Thus doña Iluminada can say to Colás and Carmina: 'ninguno
de los dos tiene voluntad propia, cosa que me place y me complace,
porque demuestra que los dos os sentís verdaderamente libres' (IV,
773). In this perspective, the conflict between free will and determinism dissolves into nothingness. Similarly, self-realisation and
respect for others are made compatible. Juan's ideal of human
perfection is not a compulsive drive towards superiority, self-
exaltation at the expense of others. Ayala was well aware that
individuals can easily be sacrificed to ideals, which is why he is so
critical of a social code such as *pundonor*. In the *Parergon*, doña
Iluminada says: 'El ideal es una verdad rarísima, que apenas se
compadece con la realidad. La verdad de todos los días es más
modesta y acaso menos peligrosa, menos expuesta a equivocaciones
irremediables' (IV, 779). Behind this lies the firm conviction that
each human being, with his unique vision of the world, is of value
and that he should be free to realise his potentialities in as complete

a manner as possible. The mature acceptance of others is inextricably bound up with feeling secure in one's own being. Juan, originally fanatical and dogmatic, ends by preaching a doctrine of extreme tolerance which allows for the greatest possible degree of human differentiation: 'Si en la ciudad hubiera un solo judío, un solo turco, un solo luterano, y éstos de corazón, sería suficiente razón para que asimismo hubiera una sinagoga, una mezquita y un templo protestante. No nos ocupemos del uso que los demás hacen de las cosas del mundo y de las instituciones de la sociedad. Cada cual debe pensar que todo lo que hay sobre la tierra ha sido creado exclusivamente para él' (V, 778). Juan here articulates a belief that is a fundamental principle of Ayala's philosophy and art and which recurs again and again in his writings. The author's creativity is an instrument of his liberalism: 'El espíritu liberal y la facultad creadora vienen a ser una cosa misma. El Creador imprime en el tuétano o más encerrada sustancia de cada criatura un anhelo simple, un elemental, una ley o arquetipo. Según se acerque más o menos a la plenitud de su arquetipo, afirmando su propia ley íntima, cada criatura es más o menos buena ... El espíritu liberal o facultad creadora procura como fin excelso y único de la vida la plena expansión de la personalidad, de cada personalidad' (III, 55).

As a statement on life, the *Parergon* directs us towards a liberal, humanist interpretation of the novel, but the real significance of *Tigre Juan* and *El curandero de su honra* lies as much in their form as in their ideology, in the blending of elements of life and literature into a unified work of art. The novel sets out to parody the conventions of the Golden Age *comedia*. The adoption of a comic perspective and the reversal of the traditional outcome of the honour play expose the hollowness and inhumanity of the code of *pundonor*. But parody gives way to a more profound exploration of the fascination of myths and fictions. Around his central theme Ayala constructs a rich and complex narrative which, drawing on modern theories of psychology, Asturian folklore, Christian and Pagan ritual, legends, and literary archetypes, explores the imaginative means by which man has sought to give shape to his experience. Individual delusions and collective myths are shown to be similar in structure and purpose: they are fictions which enable man to make sense of the world and adapt it to his inner world of fantasy. The final vision of

Tigre Juan and *El curandero de su honra*, so reminiscent of the happy endings of children's fairy-tales, in which conflicts are resolved and opposing forces brought into harmony, is a momentary liberation from the contradictions and tensions inherent in reality. It is an acknowledgement of the human mind's incessant striving for order and meaning to which the world of art gives access. The discovery of a sense of fulfilment and wholeness, which is experienced in the life of Tigre Juan and expressed in the integration of the disparate elements of the novel into a fiction of great formal beauty and proportion, is one of the undoubted pleasures of imaginative literature. The novel does not claim to be life, nor does it aspire to the realm of pure art. *Tigre Juan* and *El curandero de su honra* attempt a difficult balance between objective reality and subjective vision. By avoiding the extremes of both aestheticism and realism, Ayala creates a novel which is a subtle and ambivalent synthesis of art and life, asserting neither the superiority of the one nor of the other, but leaving the reader with a sense that his knowledge and awareness of both have been immeasurably enriched.

Bibliographical Note

Tigre Juan and *El curandero de su honra* can be consulted in Volume IV of the Aguilar edition of the *Obras completas* (Madrid, 1969), pp. 551-797. Since this Critical Guide was written, Andrés Amorós has produced a new edition of the novel published by Castalia (Madrid, 1980). The novel has been translated into English by Walter Starkie under the title of *Tiger Juan* (New York, 1933). Individual studies of the novel are rare.

1. Francisco Agustín, *Ramón Pérez de Ayala. Su vida y obras* (Madrid, 1927). A pioneering study, unrestrained in its praise for the author, which has been largely superseded by more recent criticism.

2. Andrés Amorós, *La novela intelectual de Ramón Pérez de Ayala* (Madrid, 1972). The most thorough and reliable study of Ayala's novels, by the acknowledged specialist in the field. Shows an imbalance in favour of the early novels.

3. Mariano Baquero Goyanes, *Perspectivismo y contraste* (Madrid, 1960). Contains two important and perceptive essays on Ayala, one on the tragicomic quality of his novels and one on his perspectivism.

4. Walter A. Dobrian, 'Development and Evolution in Pérez de Ayala's *Tigre Juan*', in *Literature and Society*, edited by Bernice Slote (Lincoln, Nebraska, 1964), pp. 187-210. Studies the fullness of the characterisation of Tigre Juan: from the outside through emphasis on social environment and personal relationships, and from the inside through the use of poetry, letters and interior monologue.

5. Leon Livingstone, 'The Theme of the "Paradoxe sur le comédien" in the Novels of Pérez de Ayala', *Hispanic Review*,

XXII (1954), 208-23. A fundamental study of the dualism of Ayala's aesthetics, showing how he creates the paradoxical effect of both involvement and detachment on the part of his readers.

6. Julio Matas, *Contra el honor. Las novelas normativas de Ramón Pérez de Ayala* (Madrid, 1974). Although restricted to some extent by the general theory of the normative nature of Ayala's fiction which the author advances, this study contains many valuable insights into the later fiction. Good chapters on *Tigre Juan* and *El curandero de su honra* and on formal aspects of the major novels.

7. Eugenio de Nora, *La novela española contemporánea*, I (Madrid, 1958). Contains a readable chapter on Ayala (pp. 467-513) which alludes to the fusion of myth and *costumbrismo* in *Tigre Juan* and *El curandero de su honra*.

8. Marguerite C. Rand, *Ramón Pérez de Ayala*, Twayne's World Authors Series, 138 (New York, 1971). A sound general introduction to the author but lacking in critical insight.

9. K.W. Reinink, *Algunos aspectos literarios y lingüísticos de la obra de don Ramón Pérez de Ayala* (The Hague, 1959). Although lacking in overall argument, this book contains useful chapters on Ayala's language stressing particularly his use of popular and regional expressions and his sensitivity to colour.

10. Maruxa Salgués Cargill and Julián Palley, 'Myth and Anti-Myth in *Tigre Juan*', *Revista de Estudios Hispánicos*, VII (1973), 399-416. Makes the basic points on the three myths of Don Juan, *pundonor*, and Beauty and the Beast.

11. Donald L. Shaw, 'On the Ideology of Pérez de Ayala', *Modern Language Quarterly*, XXII (1961), 158-66. An interesting account of Ayala's philosophical evolution, drawing on his essays as well as his novels. As its title implies, an ideological

rather than a literary critical approach.

12.   Norma Urrutia, *De Troteras a Tigre Juan* (Madrid, 1960). Sees the novel mainly as the exposition of a thesis and approaches it largely from a thematic point of view.

13.   Frances Wyers Weber, *The Literary Perspectivism of Ramón Pérez de Ayala*, University of North Carolina Studies in the Romance Languages and Literatures, 60 (Chapel Hill, 1966). Highly stimulating and intellectual. Tends to lose sight of the novels as novels, but essential reading nonetheless.

ADDENDUM

14.   Marigold Best, *Ramón Pérez de Ayala: an annotated bibliography of criticism*, Research Bibliographies and Checklists, 33 (London: Grant & Cutler, 1980).